# The Intentional Life

CULTIVATE CONFIDENCE,
BUILD YOUR BOUNDARIES,
PROTECT YOUR PEACE

# The Intentional Life

CRISTINA SLABIC

Library of Congress Cataloging-in-Publication Data

LCCN: 2023924261 (paperback) ISBN: 978-1-961732-12-4 (ebook) ISBN: 978-1-961732-13-1 (paperback) | ISBN: 978-1-961732-14-8 (hardcover)

Published in association with Called Creatives Publishing, www.calledcreativespublishing.com

Cover design: Called Creatives Publishing
Interior design: Cristina Slabic

2024 – First Edition

# Table of Contents

# Foreword

Cristina Slabic and her book are a gift to those who want to get more done, but it is also a gift to those of us who feel the pressure to do *just a little bit more.*

I'm a recovering achievement addict. When I was in high school, I was one of those kids who participated in everything humanly possible. I played sports; I was on the debate team; I was in plays and musicals; I was in student government; if memory serves correctly, I was even in the Spanish club. I joined every activity possible, all while striving to get great grades in the top classes. I carried that achievement addiction into college, joining multiple campus organizations, serving in leadership roles, and making plans to make grades that would qualify me for graduate school. All achievers go to graduate school, you know.

As you might imagine, all this focus on busyness and achievement began to become nearly impossible to manage. One of my mentors noticed I was struggling and introduced me to the world of the Franklin Covey planner. I learned the principles of time management, scheduling, prioritizing tasks, and getting organized. I remember feeling relief at finally feeling I was officially "organized."

The problem with being an achievement addict, however, is the nagging thought that one should always be doing *just a little bit more*. I never stopped to consider why I felt this way, to ask why I found deep satisfaction in not only getting things done but in getting things done that I thought might be somehow impressive to others—or myself.

As I eventually finished graduate school, my wife and I planted a church (in case you needed further proof I was a true achievement addict). For those who have never been part of a church plant, it is one of the most humbling experiences possible to go through. It was there that the Lord confronted me about my achievement addiction. One Sunday morning we had an abysmally small attendance. I knew where everyone was. Some had family commitments; some were sick; some were on vacation. Nevertheless, I went home and sunk into a depressive episode. I convinced myself I was a failure--that I would never amount to anything.

There, in that moment, the Lord showed me my heart. Lovingly, he helped me see that I was focused on achievement because I wanted to do things to make myself feel worthy, to feel loved, admired, and appreciated. Many of the things I was doing and had done were couched in religious language ("doing great things for God") but were honestly about feeding my ego.

I began to think differently about achievement on that day, and the Lord has slowly healed me from believing that my worth is found in what I can accomplish.

Through pain, I discovered what Cristina will help you remember: Your first identity is found in Jesus.

Cristina's book points each of us back to our first identity—a child of God who is at his or her best when we abide in Jesus. There, remembering how God made us, can we partner with Him in the redemption of creation. That is, after all, what all good work is—a partnership with God. If you are not an achievement addict but are instead one who struggles with getting things done, Cristina's book will help you, as well. By starting with identity in God, she short circuits our attempts to make our goals about us and instead redirects our efforts in the right direction.

Then, and only then, does she give us the tips and tricks that increase productivity. She knows what we all need to know—busyness apart from a settled identity will only lead to frustration. With every page I found myself thinking, "I wish I would have had this book twenty years ago."

Cristina is an expert at getting things done. You'll see that as you read her book. But more than that, you'll see her true motivation—for you to be productive in a way that brings you into greater harmony and partnership with your Creator.

That is, after all, why He made us—for relationship and partnership so that we might know Him.

Here's to abiding.

Steve Bezner
Senior Pastor
Houston Northwest Church

# Author's Note

Dear friend,

I have been praying for YOU. I'm so glad you picked up this book.

You are reading the book I wish I had found years ago while trying to figure out what it means to live in Christ with purpose and intention. I wanted to make plans but didn't want to get ahead of God. This book contains the steps I have learned to re-center my life on God. I call it recalibration (because I'm an engineer nerd).

Simply, I want to live in Him, by Him, and for Him.

When I started to look for help living an intentional life as a Christian, I found books about the Christian life that left me asking, "But HOW?" So, I searched for help on the "how to," and I found books and articles about setting goals and creating systems to get things done. Those were helpful but left me wondering if I was honoring God through those processes. Was I doing something out of order? Was I making plans and then asking God to bless them? That route felt wrong, too.

I had so many questions, and I felt stuck for so long! I went back and forth between feeling confident that I could set big goals because I was smart, resourceful, and ambitious and wondering if I was cutting God out of the process. I kept digging and praying for God to show me--and He did! And I want to show you what I found.

You will read parts of my story because God has been working my whole life to lead me here. But more importantly, you will see which Bible stories God used to answer my questions and guide me. The Bible is God's Word; it is how He speaks to us. God makes Himself known in His Word and shows us all that we need to know. It does not tell us *everything*, but there is enough in His Word to guide us and help us recognize the move of the Spirit. So, keep the Bible near and check the stories for yourself. Read the context and come along as I make some connections that I pray will help you. Being a faithful Christian and wanting to live intentionally are not mutually exclusive pursuits. Our faith in God can fuel the intentional life we want. In fact, as children of God, we have the best source of purpose because we are connected to the One who created us and everything around us *on purpose!*

God has brought you to this book, and I am honored to be part of how God might invite you into a great adventure. As you walk with God through this, read His Word, pray continually, obey the Spirit's prompting, stay in community with other believers, and keep your eyes open. I am rooting for you!

My goal is to serve the Body of Christ as every one of us leads intentional lives that give glory to God with whatever gifts He has given us and in whatever context He has placed us. All of us, together, get to show Him to a world that needs Him!

*May the LORD bless you and protect you;*
*May the LORD smile on you and be gracious to you;*
*May the LORD show you his favor and give you his peace.*

(Numbers 6:24-26, NLT)

If you ever want to connect about anything you are reading, reach out: cristina@cristinaslabic.com.

Your sister in Christ,

*Cristina*

PS: After each chapter, I will give you some steps to process and incorporate whatever material I covered in that section. Please return to whichever step you need each time you feel stuck or overwhelmed.

# ACTION STEPS:

- Designate a journal to use when responding to each chapter's concluding questions. I will call this your processing journal. If you would prefer to download a workbook, go to www.cristinaslabic.com/abideworkbook

- As seasons change, you will need help with one or more of these steps. Date your journal entries and celebrate the continual learning and growth.

- Consider inviting a friend to go through this book with you.

- Ask a mentor to pray for you as you work through the steps in this book.

# Chapter One

## WHY THIS BOOK?

I am writing the book I needed when I felt a tug to do something for God but wasn't sure what that was. At first, I didn't know what use I could be for God. I had been home with little kids for a few years, and my life as a professional was long gone. Adjusting to life as a full-time homemaker and mom took a while. I was not looking to make wholesale changes again.

I had learned to be content with my life. I knew I was doing important work by pouring into my family. We had friends who shared our values and life stage. Life was good. Still, the day arrived when I recognized I was restless. I suppose I finally got enough sleep and looked up to see that the care of little humans no longer consumed my life. I had time and energy for more. But what?

The church I attended at the time strongly emphasized world missions, so I jumped in to help with an annual conference it hosted. We welcomed our missionaries and designed events and displays to highlight the global work in which they were involved. I learned about global evangelization and how many languages still had no Scripture translation. It was eye-opening to learn what was going on outside of this country.

That year, after hosting a missionary couple in our home, we received a copy of John Piper's book, *Don't Waste Your Life*, as a token of appreciation. God used this book to open my eyes to the incredible need to proclaim Jesus all over the world. The testimonies of all those missionaries shook me awake. I was living a lovely and safe life and was content with it. But in that season, I was convicted that I was also complacent. I was hiding behind my "responsibilities" and neglecting needs that were becoming more and more evident.

Perhaps I saw the needs because I had gifts and abilities that could be used to meet them, but in my self-focus, I had only used them to benefit my life and family. However, once my eyes were opened to the need in the world, I was quickly overwhelmed.

How could one person make a difference? I didn't immediately know it, but I had also seen many people doing their part to impact communities all over the globe. Some were doing things that looked *big*, like living in countries that were hostile toward Christians, and some were living out their faith in countries that had decided that God wasn't real or relevant. Why couldn't my family and I live intentionally like they were? They loved their neighbors and talked about Jesus whenever they could. Those missionaries were the only way for people in those places to learn about God.

Here I was, living in a Christian nation but abdicating my responsibility to live out my faith. If my neighbors wanted to know about God, I relied on the countless churches around. If I had a relationship with them, I might invite them to some special Christmas or Easter program. I waited for them to ask and initiate spiritual conversations. Of course, I prided myself in being ready with an answer, but few made the first move.

I finally decided to start using my gifts within my local church to increase awareness of what our missionaries were doing. I was convinced that if others knew what I had learned, they would be moved to pray, give, or somehow support that work. I felt part of this bigger goal, and it was fulfilling and exciting. However, it was heartbreaking to encounter obstacles to this work. Why wouldn't people want to join God's work in other nations? Many didn't even want to know what was going on or what was needed. Why was it so difficult to enlist their skills and talents to magnify the impact the missionaries were already having? Why did it seem that sharing the name of Jesus with the world had become an afterthought?

I did what I could and shared what had shaken me awake, thinking it would have the same impact on others. It did not. I was discouraged, but after some time I realized that God works differently on each of us.

As for me, I was captivated by a simple truth. People needed to learn that they had been created on purpose with a purpose, and I wanted to be the one to tell them. Perhaps some were called to cross-cultural missions, but I wanted everyone in the body of Christ to engage and do *something*. Maybe it would be teaching Sunday school, greeting guests at church, sharing the love of God at the crisis pregnancy center, tutoring at the local elementary school, or providing a meal for a family. Focusing on all the needs is overwhelming, but if each of us does what we were made to do, one need at a time is met. Then we can each feel the satisfaction of doing meaningful work.

There are so many places to share and use the gifts God has specifically given you. I want you to feel the satisfaction of working where your gifts match a specific need. This is how you would engage in fulfilling work. This is a holy satisfaction you and I can feel at the end of each day, even when the work is challenging, even when we suffer setbacks. Each of us, in different ways, working to meet the needs!

Imagine the impact of all of us doing what we were made to do!

I want to help you see YOUR part and encourage you to live that out confidently. Then, it will be for your joy, the building of the body, and the glory of God!

Maybe you are already feeling a tug toward something. Do you wonder if it is God's will for you? Does it feel too big for you to tackle? Maybe you don't know what to do with that tug—you can't imagine what part you could play. Or maybe you have an idea of what you'd like to do but don't know how to make room on your calendar or in your budget.

Maybe you know exactly what you are supposed to do but are paralyzed by the idea that you are going after something with the wrong motives.

Maybe you've started taking steps and found that other people are already doing what you thought was your job, which is discouraging you.

I have felt all these things at some point. So, yes, I see the call to take the gospel to the ends of the world, and I have learned how to share the gospel and love people who think and believe differently. But I also see the need to help the people of God take their places in God's work of building the kingdom.

For every person who travels into another culture to share the gospel of Jesus Christ, countless others are involved in their preparation, training, and support. Some of God's people are called to train missionaries in sound theology and methods for cross-cultural evangelization. Others pour into missionaries' spiritual formation because they will need to stand firm in their faith. Others help strengthen marriages and families for the pressures of living in another cultural context. Some are called to pray for the workers and for the people among whom they will live. Some people are called to give financially so this work can happen—counseling, training, facilitating re-location, supporting missions on the ground, and helping provide care for cross-cultural ministers (physical, mental, and spiritual).

In this way, all those involved with sending people to proclaim the gospel are a part of that work. This is true regardless of where they proclaim the gospel—across the ocean or across the street. This is how the whole Body of Christ works together. You can be part of that team!

Whatever you are being called to do, you are not alone. Your contribution is needed. Please keep reading and keep walking with God. Don't shrink back, and don't think anything is insignificant.

You are on the cusp of something new, and I want to help you stay connected to God so that you are confident that He is involved in your journey. He is leading, guiding, and equipping you. When you know God is with you, you can be full of peace, joy, and courage as you obey whatever He tells you. You will see that not only is God with you, but there are also co-laborers waiting to amplify the impact of your obedience.

After several years of serving in various ministries and constantly being asked for help with time management, I launched my time management and productivity coaching practice in 2019. At first, I felt conflicted about giving less of my time and effort to the work at my church. It seems obvious to me now, but I had not yet made the connection that my coaching was precisely how I could help the body of Christ. I am embarrassed about how long it took me to see it. I wrongly assumed it could not be part of my call to help the Church because I was building a business. Now, I see that the skills I use to help my clients are the same skills we all need regardless of our "job."

## Coach and Minister

This book, therefore, intersects my work as a coach and my call as a minister to the Body of Christ. I enjoy helping my clients create structure around their schedules and design systems so that they live according to what matters to them. It is foundational that each of us become a good steward of our time and energy if we want to live intentional lives for the glory of God. Realtors, financial planners, small business owners, and stay-at-home moms all want to use their time well.

Because of the practical tools in this book, I hope you too will benefit from the work I do with my coaching clients. You will learn the steps to creating a rhythm of work and rest that helps you reach your God-given goals. But more than help with creating a structure for your days, I pray this book gives you the foundational steps of exploring God's plan for you and takes you *upstream*. Before worrying about the dreams, tasks, and projects, let's look at your relationship with God and how He has made you.

As children of God, what we DO is bear fruit. In the fifteenth chapter of the Gospel of John, Jesus invites us to ABIDE to produce the fruit He desires from us. The book you are holding contains my framework for the HOW of abiding. I want to help you stay connected to God.

*"I am the true vine, and my Father is the vinedresser. Every branch in me that does not bear fruit he takes away, and every branch that does bear fruit he prunes, that it may bear more fruit. Already you are clean because of the word that I have spoken to you. Abide in me, and I in you. As the branch cannot bear fruit by itself, unless it abides in the vine, neither can you unless you abide in me. I am the vine; you are the branches. Whoever abides in me and I in him, he it is that bears much fruit, for apart from me you can do nothing. If anyone does not abide in me, he is thrown away like a branch and withers; and the branches are gathered, thrown into the fire, and burned. If you abide in me, and my words abide in you, ask whatever you wish, and it will be done for you. By this my Father is glorified, that you bear much fruit and so prove to be my disciples."*

John 15:1-8 (ESV)

Jesus gave this command to His disciples on the night before He was arrested. Between the washing of their feet in Chapter 13 and His prayer for all believers (including you and me!) in Chapter 17, Jesus gave them a visual example of staying connected to Him – the branches and the vine. The five-part framework I am sharing in this book uses the letters of ABIDE to help you remember HOW to remain, how to abide.

A    **Adore God first.** It is all about Him. Start there! God created all things, and He is in control. God's will prevails; therefore, we need to seek Him first. He tells us to seek Him first because it is the best way for life to work. We are centered and stabilized when we have the right view of God because that leads to worship and adoration.

B    **Believe God's truth** as found in the Bible. We have already been looking in His Word to know Him better so that we can adore Him, but we also need to believe the truth about who we are, why He has made us, and how He wants us to live. Humans behave according to their beliefs. What we believe is true about us—our identity and our purpose—will determine how we live. If we want to live out our faith, we must believe in God's truth. His Word will guide us. The Holy Spirit, living in every believer, will move us and convict us. Nothing He shows us will contradict the Word of God. Then, we can walk in confidence that our decisions align with truth.

I    **Interpret life rightly.** Life is full of hardships, trials, pain, and suffering. People who do not acknowledge that God is with us amid all of it can interpret those difficult things in ways that make them bitter, angry, fearful, or resentful. We who know and trust God still experience pain and suffering, but we can be comforted by the truth that everything that has happened in the past is for our good and God's glory. Even when we don't understand. Even when we are angry at God. We might not get to see how everything works out, but we can rest in God's character and promises.

**D**    **Dream with God.** We can boldly go into God's presence with the desires of our hearts when we know that He is the one who gives us those desires. For many years, I set goals and *then* brought them before God to bless. This is why it didn't feel right. I worried that I was asking things outside of His will, and then I was stuck and didn't make progress. I was afraid to work toward big goals because I suspected they would not satisfy me. This one step was the first place I allowed my faith to fuel my intention. I wanted a way to check that I was working toward the *right* things. Now, I see that dreaming with God is a natural byproduct of being connected to Him. He is giving me a new heart with new desires. I can confidently walk into what He is calling me to do.

**E**    **Exercise obedience.** Not surprisingly, the final step is about what we *do*. When you trust that your dreams are from God and He has been involved in the entire process, then taking intentional steps of obedience is a no-brainer. This is where the rubber meets the road. As much as you correct your thinking about God, your identity, and your story, you will act accordingly to make progress on those dreams. It is up to you to exercise your free will by obeying God's leading. That is precisely what it means to be intentional, and you get to choose to live on purpose every day. This is the intentional life!

I am so excited you are here! You, too, can ABIDE in Jesus. I am praying for you!

*Lord, You are always with us. Thank you for calling us. Thank you for the story you are weaving. Thank you for the readers who picked up this book. You are the One calling. They are listening. Use this book as you will. Thank you that you work all things for our good and your glory. Thank you for the story that brought me here. Help me to steward it and all you have poured into me to help others on this journey. Thank you for the story that brought them here. We trust you to make beauty from ashes. As they take steps of obedience, will you honor that? Thank you for all that will happen for the spread of your kingdom on earth when we ABIDE. May we bear much fruit and make a difference in the lives of others.*

*In your name, by your power, for your glory.*

*AMEN*

# ACTION STEPS:

Use your processing journal or download the workbook at
www.cristinaslabic.com/abideworkbook

- What is going on in your life right now? Record the facts like a reporter, including who is involved, what is happening, what season you are in, where you are, and how things look day in and day out.
- What do you feel about these facts?
- What made you pick up this book?
- What has God been showing you? About yourself? About a need in the world? About one of your gifts or talents?

# Chapter Two

## FRUITFUL IS BETTER:
### How the Gospel Affects Your Productivity

It was a lovely March afternoon in Southern California as my family and I toured the outdoor set of a movie studio. About twenty of us rambled through the idyllic town square often seen in movies and popular television series. Unfortunately for the *Gilmore Girls* fans, the iconic gazebo had been carted off to a back lot that day.

As we toured the "Square," the guide recounted a story of actors roasting under winter coats and scarves in the summer heat because they were shooting a "Christmas" scene. She explained that the crew had stripped the trees of their leaves for scenes like these to make it look like winter. They did not bother with the top branches as they are typically out of the camera shot. Then, as we filed through one of the "storefronts," monitors played a scene shot at that outdoor set. With our newly acquired insight, we could catch what the editor had missed: fluffy, green tree tops visible for a moment on that "New England Christmas" day.

The tour guide also told us about the opposite scenario when the shooting schedule called for a warm-weather scene, but the trees had already dropped their leaves. The set team would painstakingly zip-tie artificial leaves to each barren branch. As we looked up into the trees that day, amid the new growth of spring, we could see the plastic zip-ties left from the last time they had to dress those trees.

Trees don't sprout leaves for anyone's production schedule. The work of the crew created an illusion for the cameras. That day, in real life, we could see what was not real. The fake was apparent upon careful inspection. We can fake fruitfulness for a time. A life filled with "Christian activity" might look impressive. People might think it's real, but eventually, the truth is revealed.

## My story

I grew up in a single-parent home. We started attending church when I was about eight years old. I understood the basics of the Gospel. Jesus died for me, and if I believed in Him, I would go to heaven one day. That sounded like a great deal, so I walked down that aisle to "get saved." It was a childlike faith. I did not understand much more than that. (I wish someone had told me I could know God as a friend.)

I remember being told all the things I could NOT do. It didn't take long to resent all those rules (so many rules), and as a teenager, I walked away from the church. I made a plan for my life. I would live a fun life, make lots of money, and do the cool and "worldly" things I was told never to do. This included listening to "secular" music, watching "worldly" movies, and wearing "immodest" clothes (like spaghetti straps). I laugh at what I was thinking was a "wild" life! Honestly, it was a tame rebellion, but I saw my plans as living contrary to God's best for me at the time, so I was "bad" and "wild."

I did have a plan to come back to God. I would repent for all my "sinful" choices and enjoy His forgiveness once and for all. Once I had gotten things out of my system, I would be ready to follow all those rules and live as a boring, old person—nothing to threaten my destination in the afterlife.

Really. That was my plan. That's how I thought it all worked.

The downside: I feared dying without the time to "get right with God." I prayed for a slow, fully-conscious journey to death.

In the meantime, I strategized how to make success happen because I was confident I could orchestrate a good life on my terms.

I learned that education would give me the choices I wanted, so I set my sights on an engineering degree. I intended to have a stable, well-paying job to fund my life. I applied to the best engineering schools in the country, was accepted to most of them, chose the one 2,000 miles away from all I had ever known, and moved within a month of graduating from high school.

Step one—check. I was on my way!

I made friends, and we had fun. I had a great college experience. My mom wrote me letters while I was in college. Going so far from home gave me the distance to grow up and see my childhood through kinder eyes. I remember how excited I would get when I saw snail mail stuffed into my dorm mailbox. It was good to hear from her, and I found myself softening in my assessment of my childhood. One thing that stands out in my memory is that almost every letter ended with the same bible verse from the Gospel of Matthew:

*"But seek first the kingdom of God and his righteousness, and all these things will be added to you."*

(Matthew 6:33, ESV)

She was so concerned for my soul! Because I still struggled with wrong thinking about God, I saw this as her attempt to *lure* me back to God. I truly thought my mom was telling me that to be happy, healthy, and wealthy, I had to go back to following all the rules. Each time I read what she wrote, I felt my mom nagging me to put God first because that was the only way to get all the things I told her I wanted.

Yet, I was committed to my mission and getting it all on my terms. I thought I had a relatively good chance of earning my dream future. In those days, I would have told you I believed in God but knew I was living outside His best for me. The reality was that I was living as if He did not exist, trusting my *own* understanding and my *own* power. I was willfully rebellious. Belligerent. I believed in God as an idea, but not as the Holy Creator who had communicated His will for my life and the consequences of rebellion.

One night, two young evangelists posed a question as I was walking through campus. They stopped me and asked, "Do you know what would happen if you died tonight?"

Almost immediately, I responded, "Oh, I would definitely go to hell." Little did they realize how often I imagined that exact scenario and did not have to think long to answer them. Poor kids. They didn't know what to do with me. I already knew the "bad news" and was seemingly unaffected. I doubt anyone had trained them for that response.

That was truly what I believed. If I died in that moment without repenting and asking to be forgiven one final time, I would be separated from God forever. And Hell is where that happened. I was living a "worldly" life, not following the rules that *guaranteed* me eternal life with God, and I was not in any hurry to change my ways. Remember, I prayed for a slow death.

Two years before finishing my engineering degree, I met the man who would become my husband. We each had prospects of good-paying jobs, and I imagined that dream future happening right on schedule. We got engaged within the year of meeting and married right after graduation. By then, the plan had shifted slightly. He was starting a job with no base salary. I was headed to graduate school. No more "good-paying jobs" to fund the "pretty good life" quite yet.

But more than the detour of new careers, we were struggling to be married. Two years of long-distance dating and no pre-marital counseling (we didn't even know that existed) had not prepared us for the day-in and day-out of our new life together. The focus of my life was no longer just living for myself. I had to consider another person in my decisions. I had a new roommate and a binding contract to stay. It took me less than six months to feel the weight of that decision. Because I had never really seen a healthy marriage modeled, I knew we needed help.

So far, this was not looking like the "good life" I had planned or even imagined.

God was up to something.

God used the challenges of married life to draw me back to Himself. My husband and I argued about many things those first few months, but specifically, we fought over the timing of starting a family. I insisted we be on the same page about God. As if on cue, new friends invited us to church, and that first Sunday, we joined a class of our peers who were starting a study on marriage. It was an answer to a prayer I had not thought to pray. In one day, we found mentors to help us and our fellow newly married peers with whom to walk it out.

We plugged into that community and did life with people our age who wanted to honor God with their marriages, work, leisure time, and all other decisions. Through this community and solid teaching, God began to correct my thinking about Himself and how He works. I will always be grateful to have found those friends and a church that faithfully taught God's Word and helped me apply the truth to my marriage, but more importantly, to my whole life.

I realized that following Jesus was about something other than the rules. I recognized I'd been His all along—even in my rebellion. He'd protected me, and His Spirit convicted and guided me. I rededicated my life to Christ, and my husband reconnected with his boyhood faith. We were baptized at that church and started our family a few years later.

## Finally seeking Him first

In those early years of marriage and young kids, I soaked up solid Biblical teaching about God from the pulpit, in Bible studies, and by participating in small group discussions. Interacting with others gave me many opportunities to apply what I was learning. I finally saw that seeking Him first was about living a life that reflected God's character, a natural byproduct of a vibrant relationship with a Holy God.

Seeking God's kingdom was not about getting "all the things." It was about giving Him first place in my heart. And as I learned to seek the Giver, I started to see all the things God had added to my life. I wondered what to do with those gifts, talents, and abilities. I was excited to chase a life of impact and significance in Christ.

I discovered that I could easily juggle various responsibilities in my church and other parachurch ministries. I volunteered at the school. I coordinated our family's social calendar around the kids' activities. My life consisted of caring for my family and serving at church. It seemed full of meaning and purpose. This is what others were seeing when they asked me for help.

I was also coming out of an intense season of caring for little ones, and quite frankly, a season in which I had felt anonymous and lost in the day-to-day call of those early years. (Once my kids became more self-sufficient, hallelujah, I was getting more sleep and felt ready for more.)

At each transition, I would seek increased productivity. I wanted to be intentional about all the things I juggled. Because I was doing things for God, I rarely considered saying "no" because I assumed everything would be okay. I should be able to do everything God was showing me I could do. Right?

But really, I was saying, "Thanks for giving me skills and talents and showing me what it is that I should be doing. I will take it from here, God." And off I went to set my goals and make my plans. I was taking information from God's Word but not inviting God into my day-to-day. In His great mercy,

I was eventually frustrated and unsettled as I set goals and made plans without Him.

# All the things

Because setting goals came naturally to me (remember, I had planned a "pretty good life" already), I was not afraid to go after big things as I was discovering my gifts, skills, and passions. Those were the skills I used to care for my family and serve in my church, but I felt the pull to change HOW I made decisions.

I remembered my mom's signature verse, and I began to seek God's kingdom. It was more than seeking Him for salvation and then living however I pleased. I wanted to seek Him every day and live righteously. I found wise mentors who taught me to pray. They showed me that prayer is always the right next step. Seeking God is never a bad idea or a waste of time. So, I prayed. Would God show me what to do, how to do it, and when to do it?

I waited.

I also wondered:

*Should I even set goals? Is that allowed for Christians?*

*Is that me trying to be in control?*

*If I set goals, would I be serving two masters: God and my own interests?*

*Am I trying to make my name great?*

I longed to be a woman of integrity and faith. I did not want to have a divided mind and heart. I wanted to be faithful and a good steward of my time, gifts, relationships, and opportunities. I needed my effort to mean something.

In my search for answers about meaningful and lasting effort, I found Jesus' words:

*"Abide in me, and I in you. As the branch cannot bear fruit by itself, unless it abides in the vine, neither can you, unless you abide in me. I am the vine; you are the branches. Whoever abides in me and I in him, he it is that bears much fruit, for apart from me you can do nothing."*
(John 15:4-5 ESV)

Nothing? Apart from *Him*, I can do *nothing*.

That is an extreme statement. I am a smart and resourceful woman. Certainly, I could do *something*. And yet, Jesus' words were clear: apart from Him, anything I did on my own would be considered "nothing."

Not only did I need to seek Him first to get all the things, but the corollary was also true: if I did not seek Him, anything I accomplished would mean "nothing." I didn't want to waste my life, time, or effort on anything that could amount to "nothing." I wanted to bear fruit, not just accomplish tasks.

Therefore, whenever I served or worked for God, I prayed that I would remain in Him and He in me so that it would "count" for Him. I wanted, and still want, to bear "much fruit" by abiding in Christ. I still pray that!

This thinking was so far from how I thought as a teenager when I was plotting my life. I had been convinced that attending a good school and getting a good job would give me security and fill my life with meaning. I craved making money and doing things that caused people to know my name. But I was chasing significance on my terms – not God's. By His grace, God taught me His truth and disrupted those teenage plans.

I learned that all things are added to me when I seek God.

When I abide in Christ, I bear much fruit.

But if I do not abide, whatever I do is considered "nothing."

But what does it even mean to "abide in Christ?"

What fruit am I supposed to bear?

HOW do I abide in Christ so the fruit comes?

Trying to manufacture fruit on our own will not work. We might be able to fool others with showy zip-tied leaves, but it is an illusion that takes a lot of work. For what? For it to be counted as "nothing." I do not want my efforts to be wasted. Do you?

Isn't it just like humans to ask, "But HOW? What do I need to DO?"

## Fruitfulness vs. Productivity

My challenge to you is to shift away from chasing productivity and instead practice faithfulness that leads to fruitfulness. Fruitful is better than productive because fruit is the evidence of God's work in you. You are a child of God, created in His image. If you know Jesus as your Savior, He has redeemed you and you are indwelt by the Holy Spirit. God also created you for specific good works that produce fruit.

*"For we are his workmanship, created in Christ Jesus for good works, which God prepared beforehand, that we should walk in them."*

(Ephesians 2:10, ESV)

He has called you. You are His masterpiece. He has you in this season for specific work. Consider your setting and the people around you. God is doing something. I am praying for you as you begin this journey.

Will you pray this for yourself?

*"O LORD, you have examined my heart and know everything about me. You know when I sit down or stand up. You know my thoughts even when I'm far away. You see me when I travel and when I rest at home. You know everything I do. You know what I'm going to say even before I say it, LORD. You go before me and follow me. You place your hand of blessing on my head. Such knowledge is too wonderful for me, too great for me to understand! I can never escape from your Spirit! I can never get away from your presence!"*

(Psalm 139:1-7, NLT)

*"You made all the delicate, inner parts of my body and knit me together in my mother's womb. Thank you for making me so wonderfully complex! Your workmanship is marvelous—how well I know it. You watched me as I was being formed in utter seclusion, as I was woven together in the dark of the womb. You saw me before I was born. Every day of my life was recorded in your book. Every moment was laid out before a single day had passed. How precious are your thoughts about me, O God. They cannot be numbered! I can't even count them; they outnumber the grains of sand! And when I wake up, you are still with me!"*

(Psalm 139:13-18, NLT)

*"Search me, O God, and know my heart; test me and know my thoughts. Point out anything in me that offends you and lead me along the path of everlasting life."*

(Psalm 139:23-24, NLT)

# ACTION STEPS:

Use your journal or download the workbook at
www.cristinaslabic.com/abideworkbook

- Why did you pick up this book? Explain what you're wondering about or where you're feeling called as much as you can. What question do you want to be able to answer at the end of this journey?
- What are you wondering? Where do you need clarity?
- Rewrite the portions from Psalm 139 (from the prayer above) in your preferred translation. Refer to this often as you go through this journey.

# Chapter Three

## ADORE GOD FIRST: It Is All About Him

*"I am the true vine, and my Father is the vinedresser."*
John 15:1, ESV

We begin with God. He is the beginning, the source, and the reason for everything. Therefore, the first step toward the intentional life is to seek to know God. As we know Him better, we will naturally worship Him more. We can only adore God to the degree that we know Him. Giving Him the proper place is how we begin this journey.

He is the Vinedresser, working for the fruitfulness of the Vine by way of the branches. We are the branches, and apart from Him, we will not bear fruit (John 15:4). Seeking to be intentional without being connected to God is ultimately a pursuit of "nothing" because our productivity will be untethered from ultimate meaning.

God created all things, and His will prevails. Amazingly, God has invited us to know Him through the Holy Scriptures. He has given us His Word and His Spirit so we can commune with Him! As my mom often reminded me, we must seek

Him first. We seek to know Him and then let that affect our lives. How would you behave if the most important being in the universe said you were *His* child?

The Apostle Paul tells us in the first chapter of his letter to the Romans that every single human on this planet can see God's fingerprints all over creation. No one has an excuse for not seeing God. And yet, not everyone *seeks* Him.

In contrast, most people worry about money and other material possessions, including legitimate needs like food and clothing. It is this type of worry that Jesus was addressing in my mom's favorite passage. He knows what we need. He will provide what we need as we seek His kingdom. It is not that God is obligated to provide for us as payment for our devotion to Him. This verse gives us, His children, the priority order for how we use our time and energy.

Seek His kingdom FIRST.

## The Call

"Why do you want to be an engineer? I have found that poor kids often go this route." An interview was part of my college application for MIT. So, as a very intimidated and unsure 18-year-old, I sat across from a local alumnus. Why DID I want to be an engineer?

He was right on one count. I was a poor kid. I had dreamed about being able to make good money and take care of myself and my family. Was that so bad? Was he right about why I wanted to pursue engineering? There was more than that.

"I want to help people."

That was true.

That is still true.

The summer before my senior year of high school, I attended a short program that gave a survey of engineering majors. It was then that I chose my path. Civil engineering was the discipline that most directly affected how people lived. I felt a pull to be part of helping people's lives run more smoothly. (Thank God for clarity on that, as I never once changed my major.) Even as a graduate student in civil engineering, I focused on transportation systems. I was fascinated by how people moved about their cities in cars, buses, trains, etc. I loved all parts of the work: planning, design, and operations. (I still geek out when I see an innovative intersection design.)

I still want to help people.

I enjoy planning and designing systems, so humans can navigate their surroundings easily and efficiently, enabling them to move about their lives.

At this point in my life, I don't help people on roads or buses, but I can see how one thing prepared me for the next. Planning and designing systems allowed me to serve God and my family. Assisting people and learning to think creatively about problems is why I enjoy coaching. God was and is using all of it.

I briefly practiced engineering after graduate school but chose to leave that career to focus on being a homemaker and mom. Where again, I planned, designed, and operated for efficiency. I set up systems, ran my home and our family's schedule, and solved all sorts of challenges with the engineering mind God gave me.

(I never believed what some people around me said, that my education was wasted. I was using it every day!)

Of course, as a stay-at-home mom, I did not receive performance reviews to gauge how I was doing with any of my responsibilities. At first, I craved validation and confirmation, but as I studied God's Word, I saw that I had only one boss to please: God. I learned to look for affirmation from His Word. I learned to let that shape and inform how I thought about my job as a homemaker and mom. Because God was the one for whom I was working, I began to redefine my ideas about pay and benefits in this new role. In God's kingdom economy, I saw that my compensation was immeasurable, and the benefits were eternal. None of those rewards could be purchased with dollars.

I wish I could say those were easy and quick lessons. They were not. However, I can see that I was learning a new way of evaluating my life. One by one, I challenged concepts and definitions concerning work, pay, performance, benefits, promotions, and teamwork—to name a few. This was the stage of my life where I reframed what I called work and how I measured success.

As my kids grew older and needed me differently, I spent more time serving outside of my home. Little by little, I also realized I had to evaluate all requests for my time—I sought to be wise and strategic with what I chose. I did say "no" to some opportunities, especially when I recognized that I was doing the job someone else was better suited to do.

## Quick Note

*If you have young kids, I see you! I remember how challenging those days were. Whenever someone said, "The days are long, but the years are short," I had to control my desire to throat-punch them. So, please hear me. If you are in the thick of things with young kids, those are good years—cherish them. They are doing something in you and for you, as well as your family. Hang in there! You've got this, Momma!*

Technological advances also showed me that physical location was not a controlling factor. I could have an impact from anywhere. Even during nap time, I could obey the Great Commission. I could write and encourage people. I could share with them what I had learned in God's Word. I didn't need to wait until the kids were out of the house to do something.

Because I could not shake the call to do *something.*

One thing that has become clear is my call to focus on the Body of Christ. I often work with those who already know and love Jesus. Over the years, that has looked like training people to teach solid Biblical truth to preschoolers, leading Bible studies in my home, coordinating prayer efforts during student retreats, and mentoring young women and girls. Even my coaching has been focused on helping Christians steward their time, energy, resources, and opportunities so that they can be available for God to work through them. It has taken me years to realize that all my efforts boiled down to this common audience. I want to mobilize the Body of Christ to obey the call on their life and not waste time with distractions.

The needs are immense. The task of proclaiming Jesus to the world is massive; if we focus on that, we will be overwhelmed. But if we each work on a piece of it, and all the pieces work together, imagine the impact!

The key to getting started is to focus on God rather than the size of the task. The story of Moses showed me this principle. Even now, whenever I focus on myself or the size of what God calls me to do, the Holy Spirit brings this story to my mind.

# Who Am I?

In the second chapter of Exodus, we read how Moses, an Israelite, came to be raised as a prince in Egypt. At that time in Hebrew history, the nation of Israel was enslaved there. The Pharoah, perceiving the Hebrews as a threat, commanded the killing of Hebrew male babies by throwing them into the Nile River. Moses' mother creatively complied with the decree by placing her beloved baby in a waterproof basket to float down the river. Pharaoh's daughter then rescued him, and Miriam, Moses' sister, who had been watching the basket, offered to help the Egyptian princess find a nurse for the baby. *Conveniently*, Miriam arranged for Jochebed, Moses' and her mother, to be paid to nurse the rescued child!

The text does not record how much time Moses was with Jochebed, but whether it was two years or seven, it was enough time for her to plant seeds in his mind and heart. How much time would Jochebed have needed to teach Moses about his people and the one true God? Would she have wondered aloud if it was him they were expecting to deliver the nation from slavery? Did she marvel at how God orchestrated such a rescue from the Nile, where God's protection and provision allowed Jochebed to continue caring for her child? However long she had with Moses, it was enough.

Once Moses was returned to Pharaoh's daughter, she raised him in the palace with all the advantages of Egyptian royalty. However, he also maintained the knowledge of his Hebrew origin. We read in Exodus: "When Moses had grown up, he went out to his people and looked on their burdens, and he saw an Egyptian beating a Hebrew, one of his people." (Exodus 2:11, ESV) Moses knew who "his people" were and chose them over the comfort of Pharaoh's family.

*"By faith Moses, when he was grown up, refused to be called the son of Pharaoh's daughter, choosing rather to be mistreated with the people of God than to enjoy the fleeting pleasures of sin."*

(Hebrews 11:24-25, ESV)

Moses knew he was a Hebrew. If his mother had indeed wondered out loud if he was the one to deliver the Hebrew people, then it might have planted a seed. This seed gave fruit when Moses took matters into his own hands after he saw an Egyptian guard assaulting a Hebrew. Moses killed the guard and then hid the body in the sand. The next day, when Moses tried to mediate between two Hebrews, they rebuffed him, saying, "Who made you a prince and judge over us? Do you mean to kill me as you killed the Egyptian?" (Exodus 2:14, ESV)

His people did not want his help. News of the murdered guard was known – even Pharaoh found out and wanted Moses dead. So much for being the deliverer.

Moses ran away to Midian.

In that new setting, life looked different for Moses. He was neither a prince nor a slave. He was, instead, a shepherd who lived far from anything he had ever known.

I wonder if Moses felt confused. Did he think he had missed his opportunity? His life had been a miracle. From the rescue as an infant to his royal upbringing, his life pointed to something grand. Did Moses doubt everything he thought he knew? One by one, Moses must have had to release his expectations about who he was and what he was supposed to be doing.

Maybe he had thought he would play a part in delivering the Hebrews out of slavery. But that had gone all wrong. Did

Moses feel like he failed? We, of course, benefit from the rest of the story. We see how God transformed Moses in the land of Midian.

In Midian, he was not a powerful Egyptian and was not his people's deliverer. He was a simple shepherd. Anonymous. Those sheep did not care that he knew how to read and write or that he was trained in diplomacy and strategy. No one was watching.

In the wilderness, Moses' confidence in himself was stripped away.

I wonder how long it took Moses to stop trying to direct his own life. How long does it take to replace pride with humility? For Moses, it was approximately forty years.

Then, one day, God called Moses. (This is the part of the story that comes to mind.)

In the third chapter of Exodus, we have a description of Moses going about his job as a shepherd when the angel of the LORD appeared to him from a burning bush. Moses noticed that the bush was not burning up, and he "turned aside" to investigate. Once he did, God called out from the bush, "Moses! Moses!" (Exodus 3:4, ESV)

It strikes me that God did not audibly call out to Moses until *Moses turned aside*. Moses had a choice whether to respond to the sign, to turn, and to investigate. Moses could have seen the burning bush and gone on about his work, ignoring what he saw. Instead, Moses turned to seek an explanation, and *then* God called out.

Moses replied: "Here I am." (Exodus 3:4, ESV)

God identified Himself to Moses and told Moses how He had heard the cry of the Israelites. It was time to help them.

God was sending Moses to Pharaoh to bring the children of Israel out of Egypt.

What?

Hadn't Moses tried that 40 years before to help his people but failed miserably? Moses had been rejected by his people and been driven out of Egypt.

From his response to God, we can surmise that Moses had no confidence in himself as the one who would deliver the Hebrews from slavery:

> *"Who am I that I should go to Pharaoh*
> *and bring the children of Israel out of Egypt?"*

(Exodus 3:11, ESV)

Moses questioned his own worthiness when called to do the important thing God asked of him. The task itself was overwhelming. Who was he? Isn't that why we ask when we sense the call to do something *big?* "Who am I?"

God answered Moses:

> *"But I will be with you, and this shall be the sign for you, that I have*
> *sent you: when you have brought the people out of Egypt, you shall*
> *serve God on this mountain."*

(Exodus 3:12, ESV)

Well, that didn't really answer the question, but it got to the heart of the matter. God is with us when He asks us to do something. The answer wasn't enough for Moses. He needed more than God talking to him from the bush, saying He would be with Moses.

41

*"Then Moses said to God, 'If I come to the people of Israel and say to them, "The God of your fathers has sent me to you," and they ask me, "What is his name?" what shall I say to them?' God said to Moses, "I am who I am." And he said, "Say this to the people of Israel: 'I am has sent me to you.'" God also said to Moses, 'Say this to the people of Israel: "The Lord, the God of your fathers, the God of Abraham, the God of Isaac, and the God of Jacob, has sent me to you. This is my name forever, and thus I am to be remembered throughout all generations.'"*

(Exodus 3:13-15 ESV)

As Moses questioned his own worthiness and what he would have to say and do, God told Moses His name: I am.

This is why the Holy Spirit reminds me of this story when I ask: Who am I?

I start asking if I am enough to do what God is calling me to do because the task overwhelms me, and God answers like He answered Moses. He doesn't tell me who I am—He tells me WHO HE IS and promises to be with me.

Whatever God is asking me or you to do, the most critical element is that He is the one calling and He promises His presence. The Great I AM is with YOU!

God is calling.

God called Moses.

God is calling me.

God is calling you.

God is eternal and unchanging.

Do you believe that? This is what gives us confidence. This is the faith that fuels the intentional life.

Will you allow it to overshadow your lack of self-confidence? The confidence we cultivate is confidence in God.

Whenever I get overwhelmed that the calling from God is too big for me, I remember that He is the one calling. It is all about God and His plan for me and those I will serve. He will do remarkable things, and He is inviting me to join the adventure.

Is He calling you to do a big thing, too? When you get stuck wondering who you are to attempt big things for God, remember who He is. Spend time marveling at all you can know about God, and let it spark worship! He has promised to be with you.

God has called you. Your time, energy, and gifts are needed for His kingdom to come, and for His will to be done on earth as it is in Heaven.

To yield the fruit of obedience to this call, seek Him first. Focusing on God rather than thinking He has called you to do too much or that you are not enough. Turn your energy to worship rather than worry.

## Step 1: Adore God First

God is at the beginning of this whole process. You start with Him. Anytime you need to reset your thinking, your posture toward Him is the key. Who He is, is the ultimate reference point. He is unchanging and mighty, the source and the reason for all creation. (Colossians 1:16) He is worthy of all worship. (Revelation 4:11)

If you want to live a life of purpose that impacts eternity, you need to get clear on who God is because he is the Eternal One. God is sovereign and in control, knows the beginning from the end, and created us and everyone around us. Who He is matters most!

Whatever God is calling you to do, begin the journey with Him. Remember: without God, you can do nothing. (John 15:5)

When facing a big task, it is tempting to start wondering if we are qualified to do things for God, thinking of ourselves first. We, like Moses, ask, "Who am I?"

Let us learn from God's response to Moses.

When Moses asked, "Who am I?" God did not remind Moses of the miraculous rescue from the Nile as a baby or how Moses was raised with the education and training of an Egyptian prince. God did not explain that Moses had been sent to Midian for forty years to develop the character and

44

skills he would need to lead Israel, like sheep, out of Egypt and into the Promised Land.

God's answer was to direct Moses' thinking to God's own name and character.

Likewise, when God asks us to do something, it matters immeasurably more that He is the one asking; He equips and empowers us to obey the call. We focus on Him and simply worship. God answered Moses with a revelation about Himself and a promise to be with him. We have this promise, too. It is found in the last phrase of the Great Commission in Matthew 28.

*"I am with you always, to the end of the age."*

(Matthew 28:20, ESV)

Do you ever think like Moses did? Are you wondering about your own worthiness or your own usefulness? Do you think that you are too young? Too old? Too focused on you? Too focused on the task?

I get it. I still have days when I focus on how small I feel and cannot imagine how I can do anything toward accomplishing the big task. It paralyzes me. That is the lesson from God's encounter with Moses at the burning bush. The answer to Moses' question about his worthiness had nothing to do with him. The call was not primarily about Moses. Once Moses turned aside to seek an explanation for the bush, God made it clear that it was about God Himself.

My life looks nothing like I ever imagined—not when I was a rebellious teenager, not when I was an engineer, not even when I was a full-time homemaker. I still get to help people navigate life, and it has nothing to do with cars, buses, or travel plans. God allowed everything to happen in my childhood, my schooling, my career, and my life as a stay-at-home mom for His purpose. Nothing has been wasted. Yet it is not primarily about any of that.

It is about God!

Seek Him first. Let your knowledge of Him fuel your worship. Adore Him. Let that be bigger than your doubts and questions – there will be time for all of that. But first, God.

Will you pray this?

*Lord, you are the God of Abraham, the God of Isaac, the God of Jacob. You are the Great I AM who called Moses and brought Your people Israel out of Egypt with Your mighty hand. You keep all Your promises! As the author of salvation, You sent Jesus who lived a perfect life, died on the cross, and was raised from the grave by the power of the Holy Spirit so that anyone who believes in Him will be reconciled to You. You revealed the great mystery that this good news is for all people.*

*Because I accepted this gift, the power that raised Jesus from the dead lives in me, and I can now take the message of reconciliation to wherever you send me. Draw me each day to Your Word so I will see you in the pages of Scripture. You promise to be found. I want to know you and worship you in Spirit and in Truth. Help me then to abide in You so that I may bear much fruit and give You all the glory.*

You can live the intentional life by seeking God first and adoring Him!

# ACTION STEPS:

Use your journal or the workbook from
www.cristinaslabic.com/abideworkbook

- Begin with God. Adore Him for who He is. Imagine that you are bragging about God to someone who doesn't know Him. How do you describe Him? Remember, Jesus is God. If you need help describing God, read the Gospels (Matthew, Mark, Luke, and John) and focus on how Jesus is depicted.

- During your Bible reading, be on the lookout for God so you can know Him more!

- Meditate on who God is and build God-confidence. Remember you are His and are connected to Him— this is how you ABIDE. He is an immovable, mighty, and ever-present God. Is anything too big for Him? (Jeremiah 21:17)

- As you praise Him in prayer, guard against the tendency to focus first on the gifts and blessings instead of God's character and attributes. Adore Him, *then* thank Him for what He's done.

- Ask Him to open your eyes to see more of Him, especially in situations when you are prone to thinking He has forgotten about you.

- Consider adding this to your morning routine: Choose one attribute or character quality of God and meditate on it throughout the day (e.g., holy, mighty, faithful, loving, just, compassionate, personal).

- Journal at the end of each day about how you saw God moving in your circumstances.

- PRO TIP: Choose an attribute that refutes something that is causing you anxiety (e.g., God is almighty vs. nothing can ever change)

**A** dore God first

# Chapter Four

## BELIEVE TRUTH:
### How To Stay on The Right Path

*"Already you are clean because of the word that I have spoken to you. Abide in me, and I in you. As the branch cannot bear fruit by itself, unless it abides in the vine, neither can you, unless you abide in me."*

John 15:3-4, ESV

After spending time focusing on God so we can adore Him appropriately, the next thing to address is the question Moses asked—because we ask too: **Who am I?**

It might not be the primary concern, but we cannot ignore it. How we answer the question of identity affects how we live because we behave out of our perceived identity. What we believe, right or wrong, about ourselves and about the world around us directs our actions.

In the last chapter, the focus on God's character calibrated us to the truth about Him. In this chapter, we will attune ourselves to the truth about our identity and our purpose in the world.

If we get stuck entertaining lies and believing things that are not true, we will not be able to live intentionally for the glory of God. That is why it is critical that we go to the one who created us and has determined our value. God has revealed the truth in His Word.

Part of abiding in Christ is believing what God says. We cannot bear fruit if we are believing lies. We have no peace if we constantly doubt that we are the right person for the job, question that we understand God, or function out of wrong motives.

If behavior follows belief, the wrong belief will never result in the right behavior. Believing God's truth saves us from so much heartache and trouble.

Read John 15:3-4 and notice the three truths we need to internalize:

1.  We are God's because of the word He has spoken. In the thirteenth chapter of the Gospel of John, Peter initially refused to let Jesus wash his feet, but once Jesus told Peter it was necessary for identification with Christ, Peter wanted his hands and head washed as well. Jesus clarified that Peter was already clean and only needed his feet washed. Peter was a true disciple of Jesus and therefore belonged to the family of God. When we believe the gospel—believe that Jesus is our Savior, we too belong in God's family—we are already clean. We have a *new identity* in Christ.

2.  We get to make a *choice* to remain in Him. God commands us to abide, or remain, in Him—we submit ourselves to His authority and actively partner with Him. He promises to remain in us.

3. We can *only* produce fruit when we remain in Him. If we are disconnected from Him, we cannot yield fruit.

The enemy wants us confused about whose we are, that we have a choice, and what is at stake if we don't choose to abide.

Behavior follows what you believe—not what you say you believe, but what you *actually* believe. If you want to live the intentional life, then you need to believe what the Word of God says about you and about how you live in this world.

When we believe lies, our behavior will NOT result in a fruitful life. The enemy of our soul cannot snatch us from God's hand, but he can keep us stuck and fruitless if we believe his lies.

## Liar from the beginning

Imagine Adam in the garden after God told him not to eat from that one tree. Did Adam draw a circle around it or somehow mark it with "Stay away!" so that he would not forget which one God had said? Of course, we don't know what he did (if he did anything at all). But I know I would have done something to remember that *one* command the Creator had given me.

According to the creation account, Eve was crafted *after* Adam had received the prohibition not to eat from the tree of the knowledge of good and evil. I sometimes imagine that the conversation between Adam and Eve went like this:

**Adam:** *So here's home and all the animals I named. We can eat from all these trees...*

**Eve:** *Why is this tree marked off?*

**Adam:** *God told me not to eat from that one.*

**Eve:** *Why?*

**Adam:** *Uh. I can't remember. Something about death. Just don't touch it, and we'll be good.*

Except they were not.

Satan entered that perfect garden and addressed Eve to introduce doubt in God:

*"Did God actually say, 'You shall not eat of any tree in the garden?'"*

(Genesis 3:1, ESV)

The implication was that God was withholding something good, maybe even something they needed, and if God did that, maybe He wasn't such a good God after all.

Eve's reply to the serpent:

*"We may eat of the fruit of the trees in the garden, but God said, 'You shall not eat of the fruit of the tree that is in the midst of the garden, neither shall you touch it, lest you die.'"*

(Genesis 3:2-3, ESV)

God had said, "Don't eat," but Eve's response to the serpent had an *extra* restriction. Had Adam added a safeguard to keep God's command? (I imagine Adam as the first legalist—he added an additional rule to God's word.)

What if that unnecessary restriction about touching it opened the door for that crafty serpent to sow doubt and confusion?

*"You will not surely die. For God knows that when you eat of it your eyes will be opened, and you will be like God, knowing good and evil."*

(Genesis 3:4-5, ESV)

The serpent didn't mention the restriction to touch. I imagine Eve touched the fruit and nothing happened—did she pause and wait to see if she would drop dead because she touched it? She broke a "rule" that wasn't God's command, and there was no consequence. Did she then think that God couldn't be trusted to follow through? Eating the fruit might not have seemed like a big deal after that. Eve was emboldened to keep going. And why didn't Adam say anything? He was right there, too (Genesis 3:6). He could have corrected Eve's reply or clarified what God said. Instead, they both ate from the tree God had prohibited.

The serpent still works that way. He whispers questions that imply that God is not good and that He is holding out on what is best for us. We are susceptible to those lies when we don't know what God has said. We are vulnerable when we are focused on the extras that have been added in man's attempt to build fences around the commands of God. This is precisely why I walked away from God and from church when I was a teen. All those rules painted the wrong picture of God.

God's true Word can be obstructed by the "extras" humans are prone to add. Then, it is just as easy to break the real command when breaking the extra rule is not "that bad." To withstand the schemes of the enemy who wants to confuse us and keep us stuck in wrong thinking, we need to know God's Word for ourselves. We must go to the source of truth so we will not be deceived.

We need to know and remember God's Word so that we are kept from sin or even from adding the "extras" that make things confusing for everyone.

> *"I have stored up your word in my heart,*
> *hat I might not sin against you."*
> (Psalm 119:11, ESV)

Looking for ourselves at what God has said is critical for fighting against error and lies.

## God's Truth recorded for us

Remember Moses and his Egyptian education.

Tradition credits Moses with penning the first five books of the Bible. A likely perk of being raised in Pharaoh's house was that Moses knew how to read and write. The Jews still revere Moses for his role in bringing down the Law from Mount Sinai and recording what God said to Moses as he led the people. God had a special plan for the nation of Israel, and Moses was God's spokesperson for all they needed to know once they left Egypt, wandered in the wilderness, and prepared to enter the Promised Land. The Book of Deuteronomy contains Moses' parting words to the Nation of Israel.

"Deuteronomy" is *eleh ha-Devarim* in Hebrew, which means "these are the words." In Ancient Greek, it is *Deuteronómion*, which means "second law" or a "copy of this law," signifying a retelling of God's laws. Before the people of Israel entered the land God had promised them, Moses needed to remind the new generation of God's words, commands, and promises to the Nation of Israel.

At the conclusion of the retelling, Moses said:

*"See, I have set before you today life and good, death and evil. If you obey the commandments of the Lord your God that I command you today, by loving the Lord your God, by walking in his ways, and by keeping his commandments and his statutes and his rules, then you shall live and multiply, and the Lord your God will bless you in the land that you are entering to take possession of it."*
*(Deuteronomy 30:15-16, ESV)*

The choice was set before them. The people could choose to obey or not.

Moses was restating the conditional covenant that was unique to the children of Israel, we have a new covenant sealed by the blood of Jesus, and even more wisdom through history and prophecy that revealed God's character. We have warnings, commands, and promises as well. The challenge to choose still applies to us today. Will we choose life? Will we believe the truth God has shown us and obey?

In addition to the completed Bible, we also have the indwelling Holy Spirit who teaches us and reminds us of the Word of God that has been stored in our hearts.

*"But the Counselor, the Holy Spirit, whom the Father will send in my name, will teach you all things and remind you of everything I have told you."*

(John 14:26, CSB)

We may have more resources, but we still have a *choice*. We can choose God's Word and the life that flows from Him. Or we can turn away and perish.

The best way to live is to learn and remember what He has done and what He has said as recorded in His Word.

Of course, there is more than just the commandments to learn and remember. We get to know God Himself in His word. As we explored in the previous chapter, we can only adore God to the degree that we know Him. Without Scripture, we are in danger of worshipping a god created in our own image. We can ABIDE with the great I AM only by seeking to know Him in His Word.

The Word also reveals the truth about who we are—how we need a Savior and how we receive the gift of salvation. In His Word, we learn about our identity and our new life in Christ.

## Why it matters

"Limiting beliefs" is a term used by Michael Hyatt in his goal-setting material. The concept is that we each can believe things that limit our potential. Many times, those beliefs are false, and we can categorically reject them. However, there are times when the truth has only slightly been altered, and we struggle to discern where the lie is. Which part should we disregard? At times like these, it is harder to dismiss a belief since it *feels* partly true.

When I first set goals following Hyatt's framework, I could see that identifying "limiting beliefs" and replacing them with "liberating truths" was a call to believe and obey the truth from God's Word. If you are His child, you too can choose to believe His truth.

As a child of God, you can:

- Take thoughts captive to the obedience of Christ:
  *"We destroy arguments and every lofty opinion raised against the knowledge of God and take every thought captive to obey Christ."* (2 Corinthians 10:5, ESV)

- Be set free by the truth of His Word:
  *"So Jesus said to the Jews who had believed him, 'If you abide in my word, you are truly my disciples, and you will know the truth, and the truth will set you free.'"* (John 8:31-32, ESV)

- Be reminded of His Word when in need of it:
  *"But the Helper, the Holy Spirit, whom the Father will send in my name, he will teach you all things and bring to your remembrance all that I have said to you."* (John 14:26, ESV)

- Have your mind transformed:
  *"Do not be conformed to this world, but be transformed by the renewal of your mind, that by testing you may discern what is the will of God, what is good and acceptable and perfect."* (Romans 12:2, ESV)

Behavior follows belief. If you want behavior that gives evidence of God's work in you, then your beliefs must align with the truth of God's Word. This means you need to know God's Word for yourself. The enemy of your soul has the exact opposite goal for you. He doesn't want you to believe the truth. Satan actively and consistently opposes God's work—in you, in me, and in the world as we seek to impact others for God.

God has given us His Word. In it, He reveals who He is and who we are. It is a weapon to use against the Father of Lies.

## Jesus uses God's Word to fight

After emerging from his baptism in the Jordan, Jesus entered the wilderness to be tested. (Matthew 4:1-11) The devil tempted Jesus with shortcuts to meet legitimate needs and fulfill God's promises.

Each time, Jesus' response was a direct quotation from God's Word. In fact, all His responses were from the book of Deuteronomy.

- When Jesus was hungry after fasting for forty days and forty nights, Satan tempted Him: "If you are the Son of God, command these stones to become loaves of bread." Satan was questioning Jesus' identity and His relationship with the Father. He was also daring Him to use the creating power of God to change the stones into bread.

  ◦ Jesus responded with words from Deuteronomy 8:3: *"Man shall not live by bread alone, but by every word that comes from the mouth of God."*

- The devil then took Jesus to the pinnacle of the temple, *"If you are the Son of God, throw yourself down, for it is written, 'He will command his angels concerning you,' and 'On their hands, they will bear you up, lest you strike your foot against a stone.'"* Satan used God's Word (Psalm 91:11-

12) in the only way he knew how - by twisting the true meaning.

- ○ Jesus responded with Deuteronomy 6:16a: *"You shall not put the Lord your God to the test."*

• Satan's final attempt was to show Jesus the kingdoms of the world and their glory, saying to Him: "All these I will give you, if you will fall down and worship me."

- ○ That was a direct violation of the very first commandment! Jesus was done: *"Be gone, Satan!"* Jesus quoted Deuteronomy 6:13: *"You shall worship the Lord your God and him only shall you serve."*

Moses, who likely penned the story of Adam's failure to obey God's command, was also moved by the Spirit of God to pen the words in Deuteronomy. Jesus used those words to respond to the same tempter. He emerged from the wilderness having felt the full strength of temptation and resisted it by fighting back with truth from God's Word.

Jesus used God's Word to respond to the enemy's temptation. We do not have any other recorded conversation. We can follow Jesus' example and simply proclaim God's Word to the Liar and not (like Eve did) engage and reason when he is tempting us.

Lest you think you must be the Son of God, let us look at another Biblical example of mere humans using God's Word to combat the temptation to disbelieve God.

In Numbers 13, Moses recorded how he sent twelve spies into the Promised Land when they finally arrived at its border. Ten of them incited fear among the nation of Israel as they described the land and its inhabitants, but the other two, Caleb and Joshua, remembered what God had said. They agreed with the facts the ten reported, but Caleb and Joshua believed God's promise to give them the land. Swayed by the vocal ten, the nation of Israel refused to believe God's promise to give them victory over the inhabitants of Canaan. Therefore, the nation's doubt cost them entrance into the Promised Land.

Do you ever talk to characters in a story? Do you warn them or remind them of some other detail that will help them?

"No, don't open that door!"

"Run! Run! Run!"

"Turn around—he's right there."

"Remember, the bad guy is always smoking. Don't you smell it? Don't you see the ashes? Don't go in there!!"

I often talk to characters in stories, and when I read this story, I say:

"Guys! Believe Caleb and Joshua! Yes, they saw the giants living in the land, but they also remember how God got you all out of Egypt and opened the Red Sea. Look at how God still guides you with a pillar of cloud by day and fire by night. The cloud is there now! You just had manna this morning! God can be trusted!"

We (if you do it too) talk to the characters in a story because we have a different perspective. We see and know what the characters do not know or have forgotten. Sometimes, we know how the story will turn out. We may not know how it happens, but we know how the story ends. I say those things to the Israelites who believed the ten because I have read the rest of the story. I have the benefit of seeing the full picture.

Caleb and Joshua, however, only had God's Word and that was enough. They remembered God's promise to Abraham,

Isaac, and Jacob—and more recently to Moses: God was giving them the land. It was *promised* to them!

However, instead of taking possession of the land God had given them, the whole nation of Israel, including the two faith-filled spies, wandered in the wilderness until the unbelieving generation died. When the nation of Israel finally entered the Promised Land forty years later, those two men—Caleb and Joshua—were the only adults left from that generation.

God can be trusted to accomplish what He promises. Not only is He sovereign and able to fulfill His promises, but He also has a unique perspective. He sees the end from the beginning. He wants to guide us as we live our story. God sees how all our lives intertwine and affect one another. What He says SHOULD impact our choices.

God guides us through His Word, which is living and active. His Holy Spirit in us guides our thoughts, gives us peace, and reminds us of His Word. I will never cease to be amazed that the almighty, loving Creator of everything in the universe has initiated communication with us.

Should we not listen to the one with the most unique and perfect perspective, especially since His Word also tells us how much He loves us? He has proved He is trustworthy. We just need to remind ourselves. He has not told us everything, but He has told us all we need to know.

Believe what God's Word says. Look for yourself and test all other ideas, whether they are yours or from others, against what God has already said in the Bible. He will not contradict Himself.

Behavior follows belief, and you can't believe what you don't know or can't remember. To live a life guided by God's Word, you must know what it says!

## Step 2: Believe Truth

Believe what God has said about Himself and worship Him accordingly, but also believe what God has said about you and how you should live in Christ. When we believe something, it affects what we do—it affects our *choices*.

As you start walking in whatever calling God has for you, you will be a threat to the enemy. He does not want you to understand God's role in or call on your life. The world is still under the enemy's jurisdiction, and he will oppose you. Two of his tested methods to stop you are sending external opposition AND whispering lies that get into your head—so *you* oppose you.

Believe God's story.

The enemy knows that behavior follows belief. The enemy does not want you to have a way to fight his lies. He does not want you to be set free to impact the world. He does not want you to bear fruit for God's glory. He hates the spread of God's kingdom.

Dear sister, let the Word wash you clean! Continually go to God and believe what He says. Study and meditate on His Word. Drown out all other messages as you walk with Him.

Remember what He has said and who He is. Use His Word to fight the temptation of the enemy. Do not engage the enemy with reason. He will confuse you with lies. Simply state God's Word—it is your weapon. Stay close to the God that communicates with you.

Adore Him and believe what He says!

Will you pray this?

*Lord, thank You for communicating with us, Your creatures, Your children. You speak to all people through creation, but You also chose faithful men to write the Bible over thousands of years. It is a unified story that allows us to know You and how much You love us. The world could not contain all there is to know about You, but everything that has been preserved for us in Your Word is true. It helps us know You more and remember Your promises to us. Thank You that we have access to your Holy Word in our language. Thank you that we can gather to study and discuss it without fear of persecution. Forgive us when we take this for granted. Truth is our weapon to battle against the enemy. He is continuously prowling to devour us. Help us to daily spend time preparing for battle and letting You guide us in all that we resolve to do for You!*

# ACTION STEPS:

Use your journal or the workbook from
www.cristinaslabic.com/abideworkbook

- What is God showing you in His Word about how He made you? Are you studying the word regularly?

- What is the lie that keeps you stuck? What truth from God's Word could set you free?

- Where do you feel God is calling you to be more intentional?

- How is worship defined? By you? By God's Word?

- What does He say about who He uses?

- What other verses are coming to mind so you can meditate on them?

**A** dore God first

**B** elieve truth

# Chapter Five

## INTERPRET LIFE RIGHTLY:
### What Has Happened in Life Is FOR You

*"Every branch in me that does not bear fruit he takes away, and every branch that does bear fruit he prunes, that it may bear more fruit."*

John 15:2, ESV

The third step in preparing ourselves for being intentional is to interpret our lives rightly. We adore God first and give Him His rightful place. We believe the truth from His Word about who we are and how we live in Him. That gives us the right frame of reference and the right standard to judge that we are moving in the right direction. The next step is to interpret all that has been part of our story as *training* for our future. Nothing has been wasted. If we haven't seen yet how things have prepared us for the future, we will one day. We can trust God with our disappointment and grief.

God, the Father, the vinedresser, the one in control of it all, is at work to ensure fruitfulness from the vine. "He takes away" can also mean "He lifts up" which is a term of continued care for the branch that is not yielding fruit. This is consistent with the character of God. He is patient and full of mercy and grace. For the branches that are yielding fruit, He prunes so that they bear more fruit. In both cases, He is the intentional vinedresser, tending to the vine, so that fruit is produced!

## The Choice

Have you ever known two people who experience the same set of circumstances but react very differently? Perhaps two siblings who talk of their upbringing as if they weren't even in the same home with the same set of parents. Or a married couple who endure a child's sickness or rebellion and come out on the other side—one convinced God was with them and the other that God abandoned them. One deepens their dependence on God, and one experiences a disconnect.

There are times when the difference is that one has a relationship with God, and one does not. Other times, it's simply that God is working to accomplish something very specific in each person. The circumstances that strengthen someone's faith can also be a stumbling block to another. That is the mystery of how God works in our lives uniquely and personally. We can rely on the truth that He loves us and is always working in all circumstances.

Additionally, God sometimes uses pain to correct us and draw us back to Him. It is important to note that discipline is not punishment; discipline is meant to repair or correct what is broken. Imagine a bone that must be set before a cast is put on. Pain so that healing can happen.

*"It is for discipline that you have to endure. God is treating you as sons. For what son is there whom his father does not discipline? If you are left without discipline, in which all have participated, then you are illegitimate children and not sons. Besides this, we have had earthly fathers who disciplined us and we respected them. Shall we not much more be subject to the Father of spirits and live? For they disciplined us for a short time as it seemed best to them, but he disciplines us for our good, that we may share his holiness."*

(Hebrews 12:7-10, ESV)

If a broken bone is not set before the body begins to heal, there might be dysfunction, compromised strength, or even continued pain. It is not in the best interest of an injured person to avoid the pain of "discipline"—the pain of setting that bone right.

If we go back to the vine analogy, we are branches that the Father (the vinedresser) prunes. Plants are pruned to cut anything that is harmful to their health, to shape them for growth, and to accentuate the development of flowers or fruit. There is always an objective and a season for pruning.

When we trust the vinedresser as a good Father, then we can rightly interpret the pain of suffering and discipline.

*"Trust in the LORD with all your heart,*
*and do not lean on your own understanding. In all your ways*
*acknowledge him, and he will make straight your paths."*

(Proverbs 3:5-6, ESV)

We do not need to *understand* God's thoughts to trust Him. The proverb simply says to trust. "Simple" does not mean "easy." If we have done the work to know God to properly adore Him, then we can more easily rest in His character as we meditate on the truth from His Word. We learn to do this, bit by bit, and it takes continued practice.

> *"For my thoughts are not your thoughts,*
> *neither are your ways my ways, declares the LORD.*
> *For as the heavens are higher than the earth, so are my ways higher*
> *than your ways and my thoughts than your thoughts."*
>
> (Isaiah 55:8-9, ESV)

Knowing God and His Word gives us the reference and the standard to use as we interpret what has happened and is happening in our lives. As we look at the past, we look through the lens of God's truth. We can trust that God is at work in all circumstances.

> *"And we know that for those who love God all things work together for*
> *good, for those who are called according to his purpose."*
>
> (Romans 8:28, ESV)

"All" means ALL. There is nothing outside of this category. All circumstances, all events, all suffering, all difficulties, all broken friendships, all misunderstandings, all mistakes, and all setbacks can work for our good. We do not perceive them as "good," but they somehow work together for our good. Yet, just as He involves us in reconciling the world to Himself,

God also invites us to play a part in how our own trials and suffering are redeemed.

Each time we recall an event from the past, we are the ones who assign meaning to it. Depending on our present reality, we can either recall only the pain and disappointment or acknowledge what we felt and move into a place of blessing and knowledge. Some call this toxic positivity. Especially if it is done too soon and to gloss over real pain. We can work with the Holy Spirit and sometimes even the help of therapists or counselors, to recognize that our pain can help us learn more about God's character, grow us spiritually, and develop in us empathy to minister to others.

The promise in Romans 8:28 is one often used to comfort people that God is using the trials and suffering they are experiencing. However, we need to be careful who we comfort with this promise, because it only applies to those who belong to God's forever family. We, the ones called into a restored relationship with God "who are called according to His purpose," can claim the promise that with the indwelling Holy Spirit, we will see all things work together for our good and God's glory. That is *how* we will interpret life rightly.

The redeeming work of our own trials and suffering happens as we continue to grow in our trust in God's work in our lives. Each time we remember a trial, we re-member, that is, we put back the pieces (or members) of that event in a way that gives meaning and purpose to our pain. In that way, we are cooperating with God in this work of restoring everything in our past. That is HOW "all things work together for good."

Once we do that, our past is more than just our experience of it, because we recognize that there are things made possible because of it. This is more than just looking for the silver lining, it is looking at how God brought beauty out of ashes. Our interpretation of the past is constantly changing because we interpret it with present understanding, which is constantly evolving as we learn and grow.

Have you ever read a sad or suspenseful story to a child and found yourself constantly reassuring him or her that it would be okay? Because you had read the story before and knew that it worked out in the end, you knew that the things that seemed sad and painful were setting up the story for redemption. You knew that trials and pain were not the end of the story.

I wonder if Moses' mother, Jochebed, recounted Joseph's story to baby Moses when she cared for him on behalf of Pharaoh's daughter. Imagine the seeds she might have sown into Moses when he was with her. The story of a Hebrew living as Egyptian royalty would have been particularly applicable as she prepared to send Moses back to Pharaoh's house. I can almost hear her repeating to Moses how often *"the LORD was with Joseph."* She would have wanted him to know the Lord would certainly be with him, too.

Joseph's story spans 13 of the 50 chapters of Genesis— over a quarter of the book. Only one chapter, the first chapter of Exodus, bridges Joseph's story and Moses' own.

The story of Joseph was likely helpful to Moses for many reasons as he grew up in Egypt, and it has a great deal to teach us, too. We get to see what God was doing and how He didn't forsake Joseph. Surely, Joseph must have known it, too. We continually see how Joseph's steady character pointed to God and His promises and gave evidence that he felt God's presence.

Joseph honored God, trusted His character, and remembered the visions God had shown him about his future. We see in his story the way God worked to shape and produce growth in Joseph through all that happened to him. God also included Joseph in the plan to save the fledgling nation of Israel. Because Joseph was able to prepare the land where they would be preserved through famine and beyond.

But it was not easy, and I imagine Joseph wondered how long it would take. Perhaps he wondered if God had forgotten him, or if he had misunderstood the visions God had given him.

## Why is this happening to me?

Joseph was the long-awaited son of Jacob (renamed Israel) and Jacob's favorite wife, Rachel. From the beginning, the generational pattern of favoritism marked this family with pain and grief. As a teenager, impetuous Joseph shared with his brothers the dreams God had shown him. Already they were jealous of Jacob's preferential treatment of Joseph, and this pushed them to hatred. So, on a mission to check on his brothers, Joseph walked up as they were conspiring to kill him.

At this point, we see the narrator inform us that Reuben, Jacob's firstborn, stepped in to save Joseph's life, *"Let us not take his life...throw him into a pit."* (Genesis 37:21-22, ESV) Reuben intended to return and get him out of the pit. The brothers spared Joseph's life, but before Reuben could conduct his rescue, the other brothers concocted a new plan: sell Joseph to a caravan headed to Egypt. Reuben was grief-stricken and at a loss for what to do. Once the brothers returned to their father, they let Jacob believe an animal had killed Joseph. The narration reminds us God was moving in Joseph's story as God. God was putting Joseph where he needed to be. *"Meanwhile the Midianites had sold him in Egypt to Potiphar, an officer of Pharaoh, the captain of the guard."* (Genesis 37:36, ESV)

While in the service of Potiphar, *"the LORD was with Joseph"* (Genesis 38:2) and *"his master saw that the LORD caused all that he did to succeed in his hands. So Joseph found favor in his sight and attended him, and he made him overseer of his house and put him in charge of all that he had. From the time that he made him overseer in his house and over all that he had, the LORD blessed the Egyptian's house for Joseph's sake; the blessing of the LORD was on all that he had, in house and field. So he left all that he had in Joseph's charge, and because of him he had no concern about anything but the food he ate."* (Genesis 38:3-6, ESV)

God blessed Joseph by giving him success and favor in the sight of his master.

While serving in Potiphar's house, Potiphar's wife tried to seduce Joseph. When Joseph refused her advances, she accused him of rape. Potiphar had Joseph put in the royal prison rather than exact the expected punishment of death.[i] This lesser punishment moved Joseph closer to Pharaoh. *"But the LORD was with Joseph and showed him steadfast love and gave him favor in the sight of the keeper of the prison. And the keeper of the prison put Joseph in charge of all the prisoners who were in the prison."* (Genesis 39:21-22, ESV)

Even though he was a prisoner himself, Joseph again enjoyed favor as the overseer of the prison gave him authority and responsibility over other prisoners. Joseph was in place for the next step, and when Pharaoh sent two of his officers to prison, they were put under Joseph's care. They each had a dream but because they were in prison, they did not have access to the magicians of Egypt. Joseph noticed they were troubled and inquired after them. He stressed that the interpretation of dreams belongs to God but then offered to hear their dreams.

Joseph gave the cupbearer a favorable interpretation, but not the baker, who learned he would be hanged. Once the dreams were proven true, Joseph requested that the restored cupbearer mention him to Pharaoh, but it was two years before the cupbearer remembered Joseph's request.

It was when Pharaoh had dreams that none of the Egyptian magicians could not interpret that the cupbearer finally told Pharaoh about the Hebrew who had interpreted his and the baker's dreams. Joseph came before Pharaoh, but before even hearing the dreams said, *"It is not in me; God will give Pharaoh a favorable answer."* (Genesis 41:16, ESV)

Joseph knew it was God to whom interpretations belong.

Pharaoh recounted the two dreams, and Joseph gave the meaning plus some advice on how to prepare for the seven years of famine that would follow seven years of plenty. Impressed with what he heard, Pharaoh said, *"Since God has shown you all this, there is none so discerning and wise as you are. You shall be over my house, and all my people shall order themselves as you command. Only as regards the throne will I be greater than you. See, I have set you over all the land of Egypt."* (Genesis 41: 39-41, ESV)

Pharaoh exalted Joseph to second in command over Egypt, then gave Joseph a new name and a wife. While Joseph prepared the country for the famine, he fathered two sons. Their names testified to the work of God in his life: Manasseh, *"God has made me forget all my hardship and all my father's house,"* and *Ephraim, "God had made me fruitful in the land of my affliction."* (Genesis 41:51-52, ESV)

The names he gave his sons showed the healing that had occurred for Joseph and that he saw his new life in Egypt as fruitful.

Cue the family reunion. Meanwhile, Jacob learned that there was food in Egypt and sent his remaining sons to purchase grain for their large family. Ten of Joseph's brothers traveled to Egypt and bowed before the one in charge: Joseph. Joseph recognized his brothers, but they did not recognize him. Joseph then proceeded to interrogate them accusing them of spying on the situation in Egypt. As they argued amongst themselves in their native language in Joseph's presence, they wondered if their current trouble was punishment for what they had done to Joseph. The brothers still carried guilt and shame. They had no way to interpret what had happened as part of God's purposeful plan.

When they eventually brought Benjamin, the eleventh brother, to Egypt, Joseph devised a test. Would they want to harm the favored son of their father Jacob? Joseph orchestrated a way to implicate Benjamin in a crime and demanded he alone be turned over as a slave. This time, the brothers were willing to suffer the same fate as Benjamin rather than go free. In fact, Judah spoke up and pleaded to be kept in lieu of Benjamin, citing that their father's life was *"bound up in the boy's life."* (Genesis 44:30, ESV)

These were changed men.

Joseph saw the fruit of true repentance and revealed himself to his stunned brothers.

*"I am your brother, Joseph, whom you sold into Egypt.*
*And now do not be distressed or angry with yourselves because you sold*
*me here, for God sent me before you to preserve life.*
*God sent me before you to preserve for you a remnant on earth, and to*
*keep alive for you many survivors. So it was not you who sent me here,*
*but God. He has made me a father to Pharaoh, and lord of all his*
*house and ruler over all the land of Egypt. Hurry and go up to my*
*father and say to him, 'Thus says your son Joseph, God has made me*
*lord of all Egypt. Come down to me; do not tarry.'"*

(Genesis 45:4-5, 7-9, ESV)

God had done it.

God sent Joseph.

God exalted Joseph and gave him favor all along the way.

God had a reason—more than one.

God orchestrated every step.

Joseph's family came to Egypt and Jacob was able to see his long-lost son, even bless Joseph's Egypt-born sons. When their father died, the brothers feared and expected retribution from Joseph. They fell before him to beg for mercy.

*"But Joseph said to them, 'Do not fear, for am I in the place of God?*
*As for you, you meant evil against me, but God meant it for good, to*
*bring it about that many people should be kept alive, as they are today.*
*So do not fear; I will provide for you and your little ones.' Thus he*
*comforted them and spoke kindly to them."*

(Genesis 50:19-21, ESV)

Joseph had come to see the hand of God in all that had happened. It happened FOR him not merely TO him. It happened for the good of the whole nation of Israel.

God still works to orchestrate countless things around us to work for us and for those who are called and belong to His family. We can trust Him amid every trial and struggle.

Even the discipline we experience is for His glory and our good. Back in Canaan, the Israelites were being threatened by intermarriage with other nations. In Egypt, where even eating with Hebrews was an abomination (Genesis 43:32) and every shepherd was an abomination to the Egyptians (Genesis 46:34), the nation of Israel would not likely be affected by intermarriage. Egypt was the perfect incubator for the nation to grow without losing its identity as the chosen people of God.

Was the famine the discipline of God to move Israel away from Canaan's influence? Perhaps. This would not be the last time God would take the nation of Israel out of the Promised Land as a discipline. God is always working ALL things for those He calls His own.

Discipline is not to punish but to repair a relationship. It is motivated and carried out in love.

*"For the moment all discipline seems painful rather than pleasant, but later it yields the peaceful fruit of righteousness to those who have been trained by it."*

(Hebrews 12:11, ESV)

After 400 years in Egypt, the nation of Israel had grown from approximately 70 people who had come to live in Egypt during the famine of Joseph's day to the millions who left in the exodus with Moses. As we saw in the previous chapter, however, they doubted God's promise to give them the land, therefore God did not allow them into the Promised Land for another 40 years. They wandered in the wilderness while the unbelieving generation died.

Even through that discipline, God was with them.

> *"Your clothing did not wear out on you and your foot did not swell these forty years. Know then in your heart that, as a man disciplines his son, the LORD your God disciplines you. So, you shall keep the commandments of the LORD your God by walking in his ways and by fearing him."*

(Deuteronomy 8:4-6, ESV)

God disciplines His children, but He does not abandon them. He will not abandon us.

## Step 3: Interpret Life Rightly

Step three for seeking to live the intentional life is to practice interpreting what has happened in our lives through the lens of what we know about God—His character and the promises He has made to those who belong to Him. We need to orient ourselves to His Truth and commit to being guided by His Spirit. This will help us guard against bitterness and a hard heart.

*"All Scripture is breathed out by God and profitable for teaching, for reproof, for correction, and for training in righteousness."*

(2 Timothy 3:16, ESV)

It is still our choice to meditate on His Word and cooperate with God as He transforms us. That is HOW He uses the Word to teach us and rebuke us when we are wrong. God wants to correct our course and train us to stay with Him. The Holy Spirit is working as we walk this out. May we be prepared to stay close to Him in whatever we are going through!

Our stories are in progress.

At each season we can rest and trust even when we don't see the whole picture.

I imagine a narrator who says, "But God was with her" during my difficult and trying seasons. Each time, as we remember what God has said to us, we are trusting that all things are working together for His glory and for our good. Our peace gives evidence to all who see that we trust in God.

## Inspired Passion

Have you ever noticed which groups or situations draw your attention? There are people and places toward which you are more sensitive. Perhaps something about them is familiar to you. Or maybe you saw God work in what you experienced and have developed a passion to share with others who are going through that experience, too.

When you interpret your life rightly, your heart is soft, and your eyes are searching for how God is moving around you. You see how the things you learned can help others. Let your insight grow into a passion that compels you. The comfort and wisdom you gained from walking through a difficult and painful story can be gifts to those who are suffering.

God has prepared you.

What is He showing you to do?

Stay close to God as He continues to guide you.

Will you pray these Psalms over yourself?

*"O Lord, I give my life to you. I trust in you, my God!*

*Do not let me be disgraced, or let my enemies rejoice in my defeat."*
(Psalm 25:1-2, NLT)

*"Bend down, O Lord, and hear my prayer; answer me, for I need your help. Protect me, for I am devoted to you. Save me, for I serve you and trust you. You are my God. Be merciful to me, O Lord, for I am calling on you constantly. Give me happiness, O Lord, for I give myself to you."*

(Psalm 86:1-4, NLT)

*"Turn to me and have mercy, for I am alone and in deep distress. My problems go from bad to worse. Oh, save me from them all! Feel my pain and see my trouble. Forgive all my sins."*

(Psalm 25:16-18, NLT)

*"But I trust in your unfailing love. I will rejoice because you have rescued me. I will sing to the Lord because he is good to me."*

(Psalm 13:5-6, NLT)

*"But I am trusting you, O Lord, saying, 'You are my God!' My future is in your hands. Rescue me from those who hunt me down relentlessly. Let your favor shine on your servant. In your unfailing love, rescue me."*

(Psalm 31:14-16, NLT)

# ACTION STEPS:

Use your journal or the workbook from
www.cristinaslabic.com/abideworkbook

1. When have you seen God work things for good? Spend time remembering and giving thanks to God for what He has done. Praise God for how your faith has been strengthened.
2. Was there a time you saw God's discipline bring you back to Himself? Are you able to praise God for that?
3. If you are still in a difficult season, where are you tempted to forget that God is with you? Tell Him where you sense His absence. Let the Psalms of Lament guide you as you bring honest questions to God, but also remind you of who He is.
4. Write your own psalm of lament. They follow the general structure[ii]:
   a. Address an introductory cry: Identify the Lord as the person whom the Psalm addresses.
   b. Complaint or Lament: Articulate the problem and ask the Lord for help.
   c. Confession of Trust: Verbalize your trust in the Lord.
   d. Prayer for Deliverance: Request deliverance, or God's intervention in the problem.
   e. Praise: Offer praise and thanksgiving to God for His many blessings.

May you begin each day compelled to act because you see that your passions and desires have been shaped by your story—that is how you interpret your life rightly.

**A** dore God first

**B** elieve truth

**I** nterpret life rightly

**D**

**E**

# Chapter Six

## DREAM WITH GOD:
## Setting Goals That Honor God

*"If you abide in me, and my words abide in you, ask whatever you wish, and it will be done for you."*

John 15:7, ESV

This next step is about moving into the future with God.

The first three steps were about our mindset – about getting calibrated to think of God first and use His Word to affect how we live and interpret what happens to us.

For years I have used frameworks from the business world to state goals. Of course, because of my Christian worldview, I wanted to honor God first but sometimes felt I was asking God to bless my plans after the work of setting goals was done. This felt out of order. So, I knew I needed a different way of thinking about goals. One that involved God in the process.

First introduced in a 1981 article in *Management Review*, the SMART goal framework was a popular way of formulating goals. It was created to help corporate officers, managers, and supervisors write effective objectives.

Stating goals this way reduced managers' anxiety over framing a statement to describe the desired results. The SMART framework was also helpful in developing action plans to meet those goals. The 1981 article encouraged objectives to be:

- **S**pecific: target a specific area for improvement.
- **M**easurable: quantify or at least suggest an indicator of progress.
- **A**ssignable: specify who will be responsible.
- **R**ealistic: state which results can be realistically achieved.
- **T**ime-related: specify a deadline to achieve the result(s).

There have been modifications made over the years to adjust the terms for use in personal goals. In one such iteration, Michael Hyatt modified this framework to encourage SMARTER goals. The seven characteristics of the Hyatt framework include:

- **S**pecific,
- **M**easurable,
- **A**ctionable,
- **R**isky,
- **T**ime-keyed,
- **E**xciting, and
- **R**elevant.

As I searched for help trusting God and setting goals as a Christian, this fresh framework appealed to me and encouraged me to think big because *"risky"* meant goals would be outside my comfort zone. I also appreciated the implied exhortation to pray for wisdom and discernment because setting *"relevant"* goals challenged me to consider other factors and other people.

This new framework also opened the door for me to consider how else to include my faith in the goal-setting process.

Before, when I worked to set goals, I worried that what I wanted could work against God's will for me. I needed a way to assess my motives and ensure that I was not usurping God's place by setting goals and dreaming without Him. In this chapter, I want to tell you how I now approach creating goal statements that put God right at the center—where He deserves to be.

God is the One in control. He ultimately decides what I can accomplish, and I felt the conviction that as a Christian, I should not be setting goals without consulting God.

It took me years to come to terms with setting goals as a person of faith. How does faith even factor in when I am the one who is charting a course toward a desired destination? This chapter includes the framework that I developed. I feel a duty to be purposeful and intentional with how I am stewarding all God has given me. What I choose matters. It is foolish to devise any plans without Him.

We have already covered that living with purpose and intention begins with adoring God first and believing His truth, especially about who we are. He has made us on purpose with a purpose. He is the one orchestrating our circumstances to train us and prepare us for what is ahead. He is transforming our hearts. It makes sense then, that the desires that come from these new hearts come from Him.

*"For it is God who is working in you both to will*
*and to work according to his good purpose."*

(Philippians 2:13, CSB)

God is at work in my will. He is causing me to care about specific groups and situations. The more I remain in Him and His words remain in me, the more I am affected by what matters to Him. I am transformed into the image of Jesus. My heart is tuned to His. That is why I can ask for whatever I want, because it aligns with what He wants. It's God's idea for me to even want it! Why would He not then give me what I want when what I want is what He wants me to want?

Outcomes are up to Him. I am free to ask boldly. Whether it is a bold prayer for the heart transformation of a lost friend, or setting a goal for a project that could impact many, I can come before Him in confidence – and ask for my heart's desire.

## Goals as prayers

I have long loved thinking about, teaching, and practicing prayer. I marvel that the God who created everything wants us to have a conversation with Him. Whether it's teaching preschoolers or adults, I define prayer as a conversation we have with God. He talks to us through His Word, His people, circumstances, and the leading of His Spirit. We talk to Him in prayer. We can be silent or pray aloud. We can pray alone or with others. Sometimes we can only groan and let the Holy Spirit translate.

Asking for what my heart desires is a prayer I am lifting to God. Setting goals is praying. And as with bold prayer, we can ask for whatever we want because we surrender the outcome to God. James 4:2 says there are things we don't have because we don't ask. What if there are plans He wants us to work toward, but we don't ever ask or take action steps? God is not in the business of forcing anything on us, including the good things that we could have or do if we exercised some effort.

This was another way my goal-setting process began to incorporate my faith. The process of setting goals is about praying specific and bold prayers. The stories in the Bible of people who said and attempted outrageous things encourage me to say and attempt outrageous things too!

For me, the most impactful of all these stories is when Jesus prayed that the cup of the Father's wrath pass from Him (Matthew 26:39). This sole example of a bold prayer has done more to encourage me to ask boldly than anything else I have learned. If Jesus, God incarnate, who came to live a sinless life to die as a perfect sacrifice, prayed for another way when there was no other way, then I can pray for God to intervene in my distress. I don't have to censor myself because my prayers are not the final say. God's will is. I will not go off the rails and experience anything outside of God's will. He simply will not grant anything that is contrary to His will. The Son of God Himself prayed something that God the Father did not grant. The Father told Jesus "No."

The Father's will was done. And always will be. I am free to ask and trust that God knows best.

## Bold goal

Who else made a bold request in Scripture? Esther. She asked and planned then took action to save her people. She did not write out a SMART goal, but she was strategic and purposeful.

In the book bearing her name, we learn of Esther, a young Jewish woman who became queen of Persia. A palace official who was an enemy of the Jews plotted to destroy the whole Jewish nation, unknowingly condemning Queen Esther as well. This caused great despair among the Jews.

Esther's cousin, Mordecai, who had raised her sent word to her so that she would speak to the king on their people's behalf. Esther reminded him that entering the king's inner court without an invitation was punishable by death. Mordecai's response to Esther has become a passage God still uses to encourage me to dare for things that are outside of my comfort zone:

*"Then Mordecai told them to reply to Esther, 'Do not think to yourself that in the king's palace you will escape any more than all the other Jews. For if you keep silent at this time, relief and deliverance will rise for the Jews from another place, but you and your father's house will perish. And who knows whether you have not come to the kingdom for such a time as this?'"*

(Esther 4:13-14, ESV)

Mordecai knew God's Word and that the extinction of the Jewish people would not happen because of His promises to them. He was calling on Esther to consider that God ordained her situation so that she would be able to intercede for her people.

I love thinking that we, who are called according to Christ, live in this day and time and experience everything we do to prepare us "for such a time as this!"

Esther agreed to enter the king's inner court and intercede for her people:

*"Go, gather all the Jews to be found in Susa, and hold a fast on my behalf, and do not eat or drink for three days, night or day. I and my young women will also fast as you do. Then I will go to the king, though it is against the law, and if I perish, I perish."*

(Esther 4:16, ESV)

It was a simple goal, to enter the inner court and avoid death so she could intercede for the Jews. She called on others to support her by fasting. In the closing portion of her message to Mordecai, we see that she was leaving the results to God.

What if we set goals like this? We can state goals in ways that honor God by depending on Him, linking arms with His people, and then trusting Him with the results.

What if goals are big things that we dream of doing with God?

## Step 4: Dream with God

What if we saw bold goals as God-centered DREAMS? Consider the following characteristics of goals which are the dreams we pray to God.

# dreams

- **D**etailed
- **R**edemptive
- **E**xpectant
- **A**ctive
- **M**ultiplying
- **S**urrendered

Remember, God is transforming your heart, and He gives you dreams and desires. Let Him know what you want. You can be bold. He is God. He will confirm if what you want is in His will.

**d** **God-honoring goals are DETAILED.** As you dream, flesh out what you want and pray will happen.

- What are the specific details of how you imagine things turning out?
- When do you imagine things happening?
- How are your life and the lives of others affected?

As with prayers, the more specific you are, the easier it will be to recognize when God has answered. This is the step that uses the characteristics of a SMART goal to craft a concise statement. Specifically, how is the outcome specific, measurable, and related to time?

In the story of Esther, the details of her bold goal were to gain favor upon entering the king's inner court—and to avoid death! She also had to act before the edict to exterminate the Jews could be carried out. Time was of the essence.

**r** **God-honoring goals are REDEMPTIVE.** As God's children, we each have the ministry of reconciliation. We are commissioned to do the will of God on earth as it is in heaven. Our mandate is to bring redemption to our domains. Is the purpose of the goal to bring healing to yourself, a relationship, an organization, the culture, or society? When your goal has a redemptive element, it aligns with the purpose God has for His children here on earth. We are each a minister of reconciliation.

Esther wanted to plead on behalf of her people. She risked her life to speak to the king about the plot to destroy the Jews.

**e** **God-honoring goals are EXPECTANT.** God is the one with the power to make things happen. Are you looking for God to act on your behalf and on behalf of those who will be blessed because of your dream? Act in obedience to His call on your life AND recognize that it is His perfect timing that governs how your life and dreams unfold. Watch for Him to move in your life and in the circumstances surrounding your goal.

When Esther asked Mordecai to enlist all the Jews in Susa to join her and her servants in fasting before her attempt to enter the inner court, she trusted that God would answer those prayers with courage and favor. She kept taking one step after another, expecting God to do His part. She knew that God alone could move the heart of the king.

**a** **God-honoring goals are ACTIVE.** Much of waiting on God is not passive. Waiting on God to accomplish His will through us involves our obedience as we are prompted by the Holy Spirit. We wait in active faith and anticipation. Moving when He says. Resting when He says. We have a part to play and steps to take as He leads.

Esther did not just pray for God to change things around her, she was an active participant. She fasted for three days, and then she confidently walked into the king's inner court.

**m** **God-honoring goals are MULTIPLYING.** If we are dreaming things that only call for our own single contribution, then are we really dreaming? Being bold and outrageous means involving others to join us in striving for big, audacious goals for the glory of God. The body of Christ is comprised of many members with various gifts that work together for the benefit of the whole. The members move together to work toward realizing God-sized dreams. From the beginning, we are also called to multiply and be fruitful. When we talk about our goals with others, some people will be drawn to join us, while some will simply witness God's work through us and our co-laborers. Then we can all worship God for what happens (Matthew 5:16). We are multiplying the effect and mobilizing many to worship! Involve others so that their faith is strengthened as we all see how and when God moves.

Esther's servants, Mordecai, and the Jews in Susa were also participating in Esther's quest to go before the king. They joined her in prayer and fasting and were undoubtedly watching how it would all play out. Esther was the only one approaching the king but was not the only one involved in this outrageous act.

**S** **God-honoring goals are SURRENDERED.** After we state our redemption-motivated goal with all its details, we act in obedience to accomplish our part. We watch and wait in expectancy for God to move us and those who have joined us. Then, we hold it all up as an offering because God is the One in control. The goal is to say, "Not my will, but Your will be done, Lord."

Esther was prepared to die if the king was not receptive.

How about you? Are you ready to dream with God regardless of what happens?

# Clarity

When you take the time to check that your bold goal is a God-given dream, you can enjoy clarity as you take steps of obedience. When you have clarity about what you're doing and why you are doing it, you can persevere when circumstances threaten to distract and deter you. Clarity about the destination allows you to celebrate progress and to correct your course when derailed.

Clarity allows you and those who are working alongside you to stay focused on the vision of a future when the goal has become a reality.

*Lord, help us to dream with You. To trust that You are at work to shape our desires. Draw us to continually seek to be close to You, so we see and feel what can be. Thank You for being always at work around us, in us, and through us, to make all things new. We trust Your timing and Your methods. We wait on You. Give us the courage to take steps that give You glory. Give us the assurance that we can be still and know that You are the one from whom all good things come. Give us the faith to wait well and continue to worship You when we don't see or feel how you are working. In the mundane and the spectacular, we trust that You see and that it all matters for eternity because we believe in You. Above all, let Your will be done on earth as it is in heaven.*

# ACTION STEPS:

As you dream with God, pray before you begin going through the following prompts in your processing journal for the workbook from www.cristanaslabic.com/abideworkbook

- To what group of people or in what setting do you feel God is calling you to dream with Him?

- What gifts do you think you can exercise with this group or in this setting?

- What will cause people to see God?

- What kind of things need to be true for you to move toward this dream?

- Who is working with you? What are the gifts that will complement your own?

- How will you know you are making progress? Is there a time component that seems brave?

- How is God leading you to begin? Take steps of obedience with what you know. Hold the *how* loosely and seek Him often as you act and rest on His timing and power.

**A** dore God first

**B** elieve truth

**I** nterpret life rightly

**D** ream with God

# Chapter Seven

## EXERCISE OBEDIENCE:
### How to "ABIDE"

*"By this my Father is glorified,*
*that you bear much fruit*
*and so prove to be my disciples."*

John 15:8, ESV

This last step is where the rubber meets the road. We finally get to see *how* to ABIDE, since arguably, the first four steps were concerned with our thinking and planning. Now we can explore what it looks like practically. How we live our days will provide evidence that we adore God first, believe His truth, interpret life rightly, and dream with God. We can SAY we do all those things, but what we actually DO will prove it. Being intentional in light of your relationship with God is what I want for you. We can each be intentional and purposeful, making the most of every opportunity that God puts before us (Ephesians 5:16).

Living the intentional life looks like obeying the leading of the Holy Spirit as we move toward God-sized dreams. I pray that you have been able to determine what kingdom adventure God is inviting you into as you have worked through the steps in this book. I pray you will find people to fan that flame as you prepare to take intentional steps.

In this chapter, I will distill the recommendations I make for my coaching clients, who often come to me at this precise point of their journeys. They have big goals and are trying to figure out how to make room for them in an already full life. We work through a series of questions to clear space on their calendars and schedules. My desire is to guide them as to create daily and weekly rhythms to get things done for the glory of God. I want this for you, too!

But before we begin, let's review the previous chapters (if you opened the book to this chapter, I encourage you to go back and work through those steps), especially since the first three steps are foundational. They pertain to our thinking about:

1. Who it is all about: God. (Chapter 3)

2. What we should believe: Truth. (Chapter 4)

3. How we should interpret life: Rightly. (Chapter 5)

The fourth step is about our faith-fueled vision for the future and how to dream with God (Chapter 6).

In this fifth and final part of the ABIDE framework, we will focus on the actual behavior that will give evidence to what you think and believe. This is when it will show if you are living with purpose and intention. You are using your free will to exercise obedience to what the Spirit of God is showing you as you ABIDE.

This is not about tips and tricks to be more productive. Remember, you are aiming to be fruitful. We want God-centered, faith-fueled intention. The tips you find here for increasing efficiency may never address effectiveness. It would be a waste of time and energy to do something better and faster if it is the wrong thing. By this time in the process, however, I pray you have some clarity about what you want to move toward. Your "doing" is an overflow of being connected to God as you are guided and empowered by Him. That is why the early chapters were about strengthening that connection. Once you are oriented toward God and pursuing His call, then your obedience is about FRUITFULNESS. Remember, you don't "do" fruit; you "bear" it. You do, however, choose to ABIDE, which includes obeying what He reveals.

## Building in vain

After giving the Sermon on the Mount, Jesus warned his listeners about building a life in the wrong way. He had just talked about how to live in the Kingdom of God and was challenging those who heard His sermon to build a life of obedience to His words:

*"Everyone then who hears these words of mine and does them will be like a wise man who built his house on the rock. And the rain fell, and the floods came, and the winds blew and beat on that house, but it did not fall, because it had been founded on the rock. And everyone who hears these words of mind and does not do them will be like a foolish man who built his house on the sand. And the rain fell, and the floods came, and the winds blew and beat against the house, and it fell, and great was the fall of it."* (Matthew 7:24-27, ESV)

When we do not obey the words of Jesus, we build in vain. We trust in our own understanding. We rely on our own willpower, and eventually, it shows. The house will fall. It will fail in a spectacular way. Trying to be productive for God without *abiding* is not a wise course of action. That kind of work doesn't last. It is pointless to find efficient methods for increased activity when the foundation is unstable.

Another key component of building on the right foundation is the element of love. We are commanded to love. We abide in God's love, and His love abides in us. We are to be known by our love. The key to obedience is to do everything in love. Paul tells us as he told the Corinthians:

*"If I speak in the tongues of men and of angels, but have not love, I am a noisy gong or a clanging cymbal. And if I have prophetic powers, and understand all mysteries and all knowledge, and if I have all faith, so as to remove mountains, but have not love, I am nothing. If I give away all I have, and if I deliver up my body to be burned, but have not love, I gain nothing."*

(1 Corinthians 13:1-3, ESV)

We can do "stuff," have activities in our lives, and look productive, but if we do not love, we gain nothing.

There's that word again. Nothing.

If love is absent, we build in vain. We are not truly fruitful.

## Step 5: Exercise Obedience

This may seem counterintuitive, but as we dive into recommendations for how best to exercise obedience, the priority is to understand rest. In adoring God first and believing His Word, we acknowledge God's supremacy. He is the holy Creator, full of love and mighty in power. Out of the abundance of His perfection, God created humans. There are many ways we display His image, but our limits are there to remind us that although we reflect God, we are NOT Him. We hunger and thirst. We require sleep. Our physical needs are a constant reminder that we are NOT the One who has no limits or needs.

Each time we take time to stop, rest, and recharge, we acknowledge that we are not God. Stopping, resting, and recharging point us to the One who does not need to rest. He is never tired, never hungry, never frustrated that He can only be in one place at a time. He never wonders what information He doesn't know and never feels anxious about tomorrow.

Each time we are confronted with our limits, we should worship the God who created us that way. Practicing rest is one of the main ways we exercise obedience. It is His mercy that He gives us reminders of our need for Him each day.

Before we can talk about obedience as it pertains to our effort, we need to understand that rest is a priority. In fact, rest is foundational. We work best from a position of rest because it is fuel, not a reward. More importantly, it is obedience to God's commands (Exodus 20:8-11).

In the creation song from the first chapter of Genesis, we observe a daily pattern set by God. The evening is what marked the beginning of each day:

- *And there was evening and there was morning, the first day. (v. 5)*

- *And there was evening and there was morning, the second day. (v. 8)*

- *And there was evening and there was morning, the third day. (v. 13)*

- *And there was evening and there was morning, the fourth day. (v. 19)*

- *And there was evening and there was morning, the fifth day. (v. 23)*

- *And there was evening and there was morning, the sixth day. (v. 31)*

Our workday begins with a night of sleep. Even now, Jewish tradition recognizes the start of a new day at sundown, especially when observing the Holy days.

God also instituted a weekly pattern of rest when he set the Sabbath apart in the creation account.

*"And on the seventh day God finished his work...*
*So God blessed the seventh day and made it holy, because on it*
*God rested from all his work that he had done in creation."*

(Genesis 2:2-3, ESV)

God did not rest because He was tired. He rested to signal that He had finished the work of creation. He also knew that we needed that example. It was in the fourth commandment that God reminded Israel to keep the seventh day holy and cease to do work:

*"Remember the Sabbath day, to keep it holy. Six days you shall labor, and do all your work, but the seventh day is a Sabbath to the LORD your God. On it you shall not do any work...For in six days the LORD made heaven and earth, the sea, and all that is in them, and rested on the seventh day. Therefore, the LORD blessed the Sabbath day and made it holy."*

(Exodus 20:8-11, ESV)

More than ever, we need this reminder to rest daily and weekly in this fast-paced culture. If a society that lived by the rhythm set by the rising sun needed explicit instruction to cease all their work, how much more do we, who can flip a switch for electrical light? We need the reminder to stop and rest.

An additional consideration is that the commandment to honor the Sabbath was given to a people who had recently been freed from slavery. The degree to which they believed they were truly free was the degree to which they could truly stop their work. Their behavior followed their belief. For their whole lives, the people of God had only known forced labor, but once they were free, they had to learn to live free.

The same is true for us. The degree to which we cease work indicates the degree to which we believe we trust God is the one in control. He is working to accomplish the dreams we have dreamed with Him. Likewise, the degree to which we resist rest shows we are in bondage to the belief that it is up to us to "make it happen."

"If you are not resting, you are a slave to something."
—Adele Calhoun

God sets these patterns to guide us as we design daily and weekly rhythms. The structure that these rhythms create allows us to build the intentional life as we work out God's calling for our lives.

## And there was evening and there was morning...

Daily rhythms are useful for accomplishing what we need to do repeatedly. They can be comprised of various activities for how we use our mornings, mealtimes, evenings, etc. Two of these rhythms or routines provide boundaries for our workday. The "edges" of the available time we have to conduct all work, including caring for ourselves and others, not just paid work, are determined by how much we sleep.

Follow these recommendations to build a repeatable daily rhythm for getting to bed.

**Choose a bedtime for yourself.** Stopping for the day and going to bed while there is work to do is to exercise faith. Like the first domino that falls, the decision to go to bed affects all others you make during your day. Do not dismiss this step because you think there is so much to do that you cannot go to bed any earlier. There have been times when I have gone to bed overwhelmed with the enormity of a task, only to wake up and complete it in a fraction of the time and effort I thought it needed.

Remember, sleep is an admission that God created you to need rest. You can thank God for each day, trust that He will make your work sufficient, and worship Him by laying your concerns before Him. Go to bed!

To choose a bedtime, determine when you need to be up, and then count back to ensure a healthy amount of sleep. Adults need between seven and nine hours of sleep per night.[iii]

If you need to work up to it, take your time and move the bedtime up by ten or fifteen minutes, but do aim to get at least seven hours. Yes, there are seasons when this feels impossible, but give yourself grace. Be honest about the reason you are not getting enough sleep. Invite the Holy Spirit to show you when you are making excuses.

If you want different results, you must try different tactics. This practice of setting and observing a regular bedtime is a strategic place to interrupt the cycle.

**Meditate on God's Word** if you have trouble falling asleep. Consider writing down what is on your mind as part of your bedtime routine. This is a practical way to get things off your mind and still be able to keep track of information. Plus, that leaves your mind ready to focus on God and His Word.

As a young mom, I was anxious but craved peace. I would repeat Philippians 4:6-7 to slow my anxious thoughts and help me go to sleep.

*"Do not be anxious about anything, but in everything by prayer and supplication with thanksgiving let your requests be made known to God. And the peace of God, which surpasses all understanding, will guard your hearts and your minds in Christ Jesus."*

(Philippians 4:6-7, ESV)

I am grateful that God delivered me from this battle with anxiety.

Remember the recommendation from Chapter 3—use a specific attribute of God to battle anxiety. This is the time to practice meditating on that attribute. Likewise, if you have found a scripture that replaces a limiting belief that plagues you, spend this time reviewing that.

**Give thanks** at the end of each day. Remembering God's faithfulness each day helps you maintain a posture of dependence and an awareness of His grace. This is how to perform the constant work of interpreting life rightly. Each day, praise Him for what He has done and how He has directed you. Trust in Him even when you cannot see the reason. Remember His character. Wrap up each day with gratitude.

Consider thanking God for how He will help you work through whatever it is the next day. This is how you cast your cares onto Him!

**Enjoy the sleep** He gives. Go to bed in peace because you are building a life founded on Him.

*"Unless the LORD builds the house, those who build it labor in vain. Unless the LORD watches over the city, the watchman stays awake in vain. It is vain that you rise up early and go late to rest, eating the bread of anxious toil; for he gives to his beloved sleep."*

(Psalm 127:1-2, ESV)

Other daily practices to consider as you develop routines:

**Connect with God.** This does not need to be lengthy or complicated, but simply a commitment to *abide*. Schedule time daily to connect with God through the reading of His Word and prayer. Worship Him, thank Him, and ask Him for help with whatever your day will bring. Meditate on His Word throughout the day. Recalibrating first thing in the morning will prepare you for whatever comes your way.

Whether you have time and energy to only read the verse of the day in the bathroom as you brush your teeth or can sit in the stillness to dive into God's Word, do connect with the One who created you and wants to guide you every day. It's up to you to invite Him into your day. Remember, God will never force anything onto you, including intimacy with Him. Yet, He is always present, and you can begin a conversation with Him at any moment.

**Care for yourself.** Whatever the day holds for you, YOU will be there. You are the common denominator. Self-care is what gets you ready to accomplish the plans you have made—or handle the interruptions God sends. Resist the narrative that self-care is selfish. Intuitively, we know that we are no use to anyone if we are unhealthy in any area.

When Jesus was asked what the greatest commandment in the Law was, He answered:

*"You shall love the Lord your God with all your heart*
*and with all your soul and with all your mind.*
*This is the great and first commandment. And a second is like it:*
*You shall love your neighbor as yourself."*

(Matthew 22:37-39, ESV)

Loving God with your whole being is obedience, but you can only love others to the measure that you love yourself. To love people around you, you need to love and care for yourself, so you can focus on them. Ironically, when you try to love others at the expense of your own care, you might be distracted and deterred by issues related to your neglected physical, mental, and emotional health. Self-care is how you *prepare* to love others well.

**Faithfully work** where God has put you. This is the highly personal step of doing what God has shown you to do in this season. I recommend creating a weekly time-use plan. Although each day may be different from another, you can utilize the power of routine to be efficient for the week. See the next section on weekly rhythms.

**As you are able, schedule time for the dreams God has given you.** Make room on your calendar to be able to take steps of obedience. There are seasons when you will only have the margins, but don't neglect small beginnings.

## Six days you shall labor, and do all your work, but the seventh day is a Sabbath.

Planning in seven-day increments gives you the ability to harness the power of habit at a different level. Rather than do all things on all days, you can dedicate larger blocks of time to focus on specific work and capture momentum. This will allow you to distribute the work over six days so that you are able to honor God on the Sabbath!

Create a weekly time-use plan (also known as an ideal week or time-block schedule). This is not a rigid contract for how you will use your time but a suggested structure to ensure all the work you deem important gets attention. This is highly individualized work.

Remember, you can repeat this process whenever your circumstances change. Follow the steps listed below.

As I coach my clients, this template helps them get back on track after interruptions. You too will know what to do when you are able to jump back in. You learn to trust the cyclical nature of the plan. You are assigning time for all the things that matter. As you work through the week, each area will get its attention.

Draw on God's strength and guidance. Pray for His wisdom as you create a template for how you will spend each of your days. Follow these steps to create your weekly time-use template.

1. Your life is multifaceted. You play a different role in each relationship. The demands on your time and energy level vary according to these roles. Sometimes, these demands compete with one another. This exercise will help you schedule your priorities. For each of your roles, identify what you need to do each day (or each week). Examples of roles: spouse, parent, employee, boss, friend, mentor, teacher, encourager, etc. Identify what you typically do—and perhaps what you WANT to do!

2. Evaluate each of the recurring and one-time responsibilities you just listed. Use the Eisenhower Matrix to sort tasks and assignments as:

   a. Important and Urgent
   b. Important and Not Urgent
   c. Not Important and Urgent
   d. Not Important and Not Urgent

   Beware that this tool can be used to justify neglect of what might be considered ministry. Yes, honestly determine what is important to you, but also be open to seeing that loving others sometimes involves doing things that we classify as not important because they are not strictly advancing our personal goals. A task may be important simply because it nurtures an important relationship.

3. Schedule work time to tend to and accomplish the work for each role. Again, be aware of the roles that require a varied level of commitment from you. Put them into your plan in this priority order. For instance,

you are the only one who can fulfill certain roles—no one else is able to do the work. This is the step where your own self-care is scheduled. No one else can work for your health. You are a priority!

Do not neglect the responsibilities for these unique-to-you roles by spending time doing work that OTHER people can do. You are not the only employee or volunteer. Even leadership roles will eventually pass from one person to another. Pray for wisdom to balance what you schedule into your plan with what you intentionally delegate.

"What gets scheduled gets done."
—Michael Hyatt

Create blocks of time that align with your season and the call on your life. This includes carving out time for the important work of taking steps toward your God-given dreams. Often, these non-urgent activities are the ones that suffer because of the urgent demands on your time.

Every "yes" to one thing is a "no" to another. We have finite hours each day and each week. Say "no" to opportunities that do not line up with the season you are in or the dreams you are pursuing. Be discerning with what you allow onto your schedule.

This is the crux of time management. Pre-decide to use the time for the important work instead of letting less important work hijack your day. You will be a good steward of your time and energy when you make good plans for the glory of God.

*"But he who is noble plans noble things."*

(Isaiah 32:8a, ESV)

4. Reserve margin for the interruptions of life. We know that God is the One in control. As with white space on a page, you need open space on each day's agenda. Margin allows you to stay flexible and move your plans around as you respond to divine appointments. This is also a way you hold your plans with an open hand, knowing that God is the One who directs the day.

*"The heart of man plans his way,*
*but the LORD establishes his steps."*

(Proverbs 16:9, ESV)

Yes, margin allows you enough time to return to your scheduled tasks after an interruption, but it also shows that you believe that it is ultimately God's work that will advance your dreams—not your own striving.

*"Many are the plans in the mind of a man,*
*but it is the purpose of the LORD that will stand."*

(Proverbs 19:21, ESV)

5. Schedule weekly planning time. A weekly rhythm of evaluating and strategic planning is necessary to take your God-breathed dreams and discern manageable steps. During this time, celebrate progress and adjust the strategy as you learn what to do and what to avoid. Evaluate new requests for your time. Each week, the intention is to ABIDE.

6. Observe a day each week to rest and worship God. This is important for maintaining your connection to Him. Stop your striving. Rest. Trust. Worship. He is God; you are not. Be purposeful and intentional.

## Begin Each Day on Purpose

Throughout each day, your goal is to walk in step with the Spirit. Do not run ahead because you think you have figured out what He's doing. You also can't just sit and wait for Him to act—He invites you to participate.

You *can* live the intentional life!

## ACTION STEPS:

In your processing journal or workbooks from www.cristinaslabic.com/abideworkbook, work through the steps in this chapter. Pause and pray for each one. It is particularly helpful to share decisions with an accountability partner.

- Decide when you will go to bed and set an alarm. Leave things ready for the morning.

- Decide when you will get out of bed and set an alarm.

- Create a template for how you will use each day of your week. A blank weekly template is included in the workbook.

- Schedule a half day for quarterly planning to revisit all these decisions.

**A** dore God first

**B** elieve truth

**I** nterpret life rightly

**D** ream with God

**E** xercise obedience

# Chapter Eight

## NOW WHAT?
### Go and Bear Fruit

*"You did not choose me, but I chose you and appointed you that you should go and bear fruit and that your fruit should abide, so that whatever you ask the Father in my name, he may give it to you. These things I command you, so that you will love one another."*

John 15:16-17, ESV

Now the battle begins.

The reality of your life and all that you juggle is about to come rushing back into this space you have created to process with God. You have dreamed with God, and you have drafted a plan for getting things done. But no one else in your life has done this work to adjust their thinking. They haven't changed their expectations. You are also about to discover the strength of your existing habits. You will feel the pull to do what you have always done.

In *The 4 Disciplines of Execution*, the authors introduce a metaphor for the time and energy already used to maintain the normal pace of life.[iv] They call it the whirlwind. Imagine swirling wind and force exerted on anything caught in its way. This is the resistance and the main threat to accomplishing important goals. You get sucked into a whirlwind and stuck going through the same motions over and over. Your challenge is to escape and make progress on goals that are outside of the day-to-day.

This closing chapter will give you a few more tools for integrating your life with this new work so you can begin each day on purpose and build the intentional life.

How can you bear fruit in the whirlwind of everyday life?

How can you step out to work on new things God is calling you to do? You must escape the pull of the whirlwind and make deliberate changes to the status quo.

## Weekly Objectives

Working to create your weekly time-use plan is done outside of the whirlwind. This plan will help you manage the pressing matters of life AND make room for the dream you are pursuing. Life is not predictable, and you will experience interruptions and disruptions in any plan you make, whether it is for the day or the week. Having a weekly view of your time commitments and available margin will help you make wise decisions about how to shift things around.

The weekly-time use plan is what you would do if nothing ever came up to disrupt it. The goal is not to force compliance but to provide the structure to which you can return after anything unexpected comes up. You can expect disruptions because the reality is that life is a series of interruptions. That is what we call them, of course. From God's perspective, he is working and weaving your life with others and thus everyone's plans will be affected. When this happens, you get to make decisions to prioritize certain tasks over others. To make these decisions and stay focused on what you have deemed important, you need to get clear on a few objectives for the week. The key is to tie these few weekly objectives to the major roles and goals you identified for the current season or quarter. Do not choose too many objectives as this will dilute your focus.

Two or three weekly objectives give you the clarity you need to re-focus your days each time an interruption takes you off course. When push comes to shove, what tasks will you have to move to another day or week to make time for what matters more at that moment?

## Daily Priority Tasks

Likewise, identifying three clearly actionable tasks each day will keep you moving toward accomplishing the weekly objectives. This simple practice can help you battle overwhelm and the temptation to give your time and energy to less meaningful but easier work.

Determine what three things will allow you to call each day a good day. When you identify these three tasks, you define "success" for your day. The goal is to give your best effort to accomplish three daily priorities. Once you do, you can celebrate that you are being purposeful and intentional. If you then want to consider additional tasks, you are free to do so, but those tasks no longer have the power to make you feel guilty if they are not accomplished. Those were *extra* to an already-successful day. This mindset shift will increase your confidence in your ability to get things done.

Maybe you are familiar with this scenario, you start the week with a 20-item to-do list. Each time you look at it, you must decide which item to work on. The ones you don't choose feel like tasks you are neglecting. At the end of your day, you see the "not done" list as a source of shame and guilt because you're not getting to all of it. You can't even see, much less celebrate, that there were some items marked off! Your sleep is probably compromised because all that is undone keeps swirling in your head, and you're already overwhelmed about the next day.

Compare that scenario to the one where you start each day with a three-item, to-do list. These are the most strategic tasks related to the goals you have for the week. Even if most of your time is taken up by the whirlwind, you have pre-decided which three things need your time and attention. You are focused and productive because you are not using mental energy to make decisions about how to use any discretionary time. Each night, you recognize the "wins" and feel energized by your progress. At the end of the six-day work week, you will have accomplished at least 18 items, more if you had extra time or energy any day that week.

This is the power of intention and focus, connecting the dreams God has given you to weekly and daily actions. My challenge to you is to identify tasks that are the small steps that will move you forward and toward your dreams. Some tasks will only get attention if you designate them as priority tasks. Stop burying them amid a long list of easier, low-leverage tasks.

# The Art of Saying "No"

Living with intention will require that you re-negotiate some of your existing commitments and delegate responsibilities to others. With wisdom and discernment, of course, you will need to say "no" gently and kindly to any opportunity that would take time to nurture what is important to you.

I joke that I am also a "no" coach because of how often I help people turn down additional demands on their time. I help them with language that honors the person asking but lovingly holds a boundary. It takes practice, but trust that you will sharpen your skill as you consistently decline requests that compromise your stated priorities.

The conviction to be able to do this comes from the work you have done to put God first and recognize that it is all about Him. Take the time to pray for each invitation and opportunity, and trust that He will guide you. I am not suggesting you say "no" to everything, rather suggesting that you be wise as you consider additional commitments.

As you understand what you are doing, others may resonate with your dreams and priorities and seek to collaborate with you. Some may want to join you in your dream or join forces in some way. Kingdom collaboration is a wonderful way to combine our gifts—we are not in competition with one another!

It is also possible that some people will see you making progress and being effective and will want your help in making progress for *their* project or dream. They will be checking if you fit what they need. This will be a test of your humility— to join a dream or ministry someone else has launched. Pray as you field these requests because this may be the way God is leading you to the outcome you desire. Ask questions to understand what they are doing and what they need from you. Tell them you will pray and then truly pray. Thoughtfully and prayerfully consider what is being asked of you so that you honor the person who is presenting the opportunity. Joining them may get you closer to your God-given dream.

If it is clear that it would be a distraction, courageously and kindly say "no."

Whether you are asking people to join you or considering people's requests for your help, it is up to you to discern your next steps as you walk with God. Consistent study and meditation on truth from God's Word will prepare you to consider such requests. Adore God first and believe His truth as you seek guidance through His Word, prayer, leading of the Holy Spirit, and wise counsel from other believers. Your identity is never about *where* you spend your time and energy. "People pleasing" is exhausting because it disconnects your work from the fuel of passion and from the vision of work God calls and prepares you to do. Working to please people will likely lead to burnout.

If you need another reason to be selective in which assignments you accept, think about this. When you take a role or job that does not quite fit you, you take that opportunity from someone else. Trust God and pray for all involved in the search. When something doesn't fit, say "no." God might be working to increase the faith of the person asking. God might be setting up the conditions to connect him or her with someone praying for an opportunity to use his or her gifts.

Of course, if God leads you to say "yes," jump in!

## Grace for Hearing "No"

Remember this, too, as you ask others to join YOU in what you are doing. You *will* need the help and contribution of others to accomplish the goals God has placed on your heart. As you identify gifts to complement yours, God will show you whom to ask. Asking others to join you is inviting them into a God-given dream that is bigger than one person. We can't do it alone—we need one another!

When you see gifts in people that might serve to complement yours, pray for additional confirmation and ask them to consider collaboration. Trust that they are doing their part to seek wisdom from God whether to join you or not. Do not make decisions for others. It is unwise to assume they cannot or do not want to join you. God may be using your request to give them direction. Your job is to present the opportunity, not to convince them. Trust God to work!

Do not pressure them or shame them to take on a commitment or responsibility if they are saying "no." Leave the door open if they ever change their mind. Remember, God's timing is perfect.

## Begin!

Life is busy and pulls us in many directions. My prayer for you is that you will make time (with the weekly time-use plan) and stay focused (weekly objectives and daily priority tasks) on the dream God has given you—even as you tend to the responsibilities of your season.

You ABIDE when you continually practice all the steps. You reconnect with the work you have done to adore God first, meditate on His truth, and ensure your behavior follows what you are learning—what you believe. Continually interpret your life circumstances through the lens of your identity as God's child. Pray continually as you chase the dream He has put in your heart, ask for guidance, and wait on God's timing and equipping. Then, plan and take steps of obedience. Look for co-laborers to share the work and blessings!

As the circumstances in your life change, you will have more or less time to devote to the dream God has given you. The call to be present in another area might be stronger. Stay connected to God by repeating the steps in this book. Then, gradually, create days that take you toward your God-given dreams.

It is possible to begin each day on purpose and live the intentional life where you are confident in God to guide and equip you.

God bless you!

# ACTION STEPS:

Follow these steps each day and each week. Go to www.cristinaslabic.com/abideworkbook for a printable version of these prompts to use during your daily debriefs and weekly planning times.

- As you plan for each week, gather all tasks that need to be addressed that week.
  - Look at your goals and projects, family calendars, and whatever else is asking for your time.
  - As you survey all that needs to happen, are there themes surfacing? Identify the weekly objectives.
  - Schedule tasks based on your weekly time-use template so that you meet your weekly objectives.
- At the end of each day, celebrate what you have accomplished!
  - Plan your daily priority tasks for the next day. Remember that each day begins the night before and identify what three tasks you want to celebrate accomplishing the following night.
  - If you are unclear on which ones, pray for God to give you peace in the morning.
- Begin each day with three priority tasks.
- Work your time-use plan as closely as you can— returning to the structure whenever you get interrupted.
- How can you build boundaries to protect your most important work?
- Return to any of the steps in this book whenever your circumstances change.

# Acknowledgments

Jesus, You are the beginning and the end. All comes from you and is for you. You hold all things together. Thank you for thinking of me, choosing me, delighting over me. May all my words glorify you.

Mike, it was no accident, me finding you. I thank God for you, for us, for our family. You are my biggest supporter—you believe in me before I do. Thank you for loving me and being on my team—as we fight for a great marriage, pour into our kids, and aim to make an impact in this world for Jesus' sake. I love our life!

Alex, Michael, and Sophia, I am so proud to be your mom. Each of you is finding your way in this world and I trust Jesus with your lives. Draw near to Him—that's my best advice. Thanks for letting me coach you sometimes now that you're grown, and for your grace and patience. I will always love you.

My friends—especially the Book Prayer Team, thank you for praying and for requesting updates, for cheering me on, and for being genuinely excited about this project. You have reminded me why I wanted to get this message out to the world. I am blessed by your love for me. Alicia Ellison, you most of all have seen the struggle to get this book done and I thank God for all you have done to help me. Jody Janz, thank you for listening to my heart and checking that my words matched. Steve Bezner, my friend and now pastor, thank you for writing the foreword and encouraging me to use my gifts to build up the Body of Christ.

The Called Creatives Publishing team, thank you for your gentle but also firm nudges to keep taking steps. Steph Kingery and Melody Belotte, thank you for managing this project and answering my questions. Sarah Farish and Morgan Strehlow, thank you for using your gifts to make this work better. Lisa Whittle and Alli Worthington, thank you for your courage and vision to launch Called Creatives and then Called Creatives Publishing. I have been resourced and empowered by the training and coaching you have provided—but more importantly, you have nurtured a community where I have found "my people." Alli, your help as my coach has been invaluable in finishing this book and in strengthening my coaching and speaking. I am excited for what's next!

My called sisters in the Called Creatives community and elsewhere in ministry, this book is for YOU. My call is to help the Body of Christ use their time, talents, and treasure for the sake of Jesus. Thinking of you has fueled this journey. Imagine if we were all trusting God as we walked in obedience to His leadership, ministering by the power of the Holy Spirit, loving Him, and loving people. I pray you will learn to ABIDE in Him, dream God-size dreams, and then live faithfully surrendered to His will—God's got you! May we all be set free for kingdom impact because we are being called for such a time as this. Let's go, ladies!

# Endnotes

[i] https://scholarlycommons.law.northwestern.edu/cgi/view-content.cgi?article=1277&context=jclc

[ii] https://annarborvineyard.org/participate/spiritual-forma-tion/writing-a-psalm-of-lament/

[iii] https://www.sleepfoundation.org/how-sleep-works/how-much-sleep-do-we-really-need#:~:text=National%20Sleep%20Foundation%20guidelines1,to%208%20hours%20per%20night.

[iv] Chris McChesney, Sean Covey, and Jim Huling. *The 4 Disciplines of Execution: Achieving Your Wildly Important Goals*, Free Press, 2012

www.ingramcontent.com/pod-product-compliance
Lightning Source LLC
Chambersburg PA
CBHW031423120626
46545CB00006B/2257